BEAN LOVERS
COOK BOOK

D0150832

by

Shayne K. Fischer

GOLDEN WEST ☼ PUBLISHERS

Cover photos courtesy Kokopelli's Kitchen, Phoenix, Arizona
Interior art by Shayne K. Fischer

Other books by Shayne K. Fischer:

Low Fat Mexican Recipes
Vegi-Mex Vegetarian Mexican Recipes
Wholly Frijoles! The Whole Bean Cook Book

Anasazi Beans® is trademarked to Adobe Milling Co., Inc., Dove Creek, CO

Miscellaneous bean facts courtesy of the American Dry Bean Board and Nebraska Dry Bean Growers Association.

Printed in the United States of America

ISBN #1-885590-79-2

Copyright ©1999 by Shayne K. Fischer. All rights reserved. This book or any portion thereof, may not be reproduced in any form, except for review purposes, without the written permission of the publisher.

Information in this book is deemed to be authentic and accurate by author and publisher. However, they disclaim any liability incurred in connection with the use of information appearing in this book.

Golden West Publishers, Inc.
4113 N. Longview Ave.
Phoenix, AZ 85014, USA
(602) 265-4392

BEAN LOVERS COOK BOOK

Table of Contents

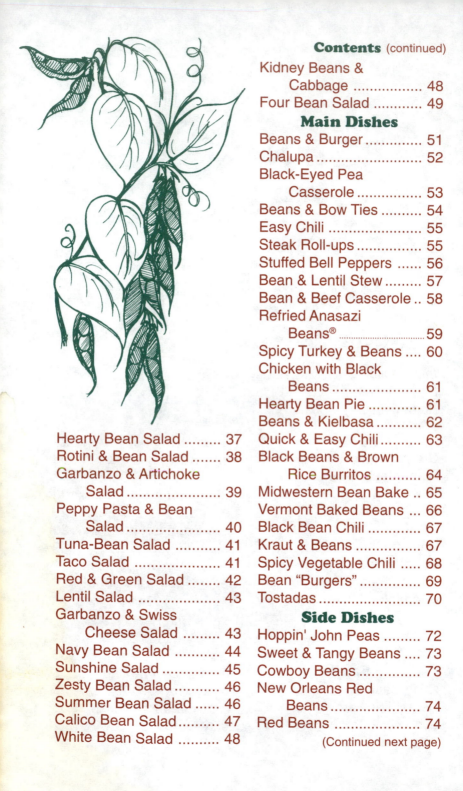

Contents (continued)

(Continued next page)

Contents (continued)

Breads

Desserts

Introduction

This cook book features bean recipes from the entire country. The tasty and nutritious recipes throughout **Bean Lovers Cook Book** show that beans are more than just a side dish or a filler. In fact, beans can be used in appetizers, breads, salads, soups, main dishes, side dishes and desserts!

Beans are legumes (leg yooms), the seed pods of any of the plants that belong to the pea or *Leguminosae* family. The pod, such as that of the pea or bean, splits into two valves with the seeds attached to the lower edge of one of the valves.

Legumes grow in most parts of the world and make up the second largest family of flowering plants. Botanists recognize over 13,000 species of legumes which vary widely and may be found in the form of trees, shrubs or herbs. Many are climbing plants. Such legumes as peas, beans and peanuts are very valuable as nutritional foods, providing protein, calcium, phosphorous, vitamins and other nutrients. Alfalfa and clover are important pasture plant legumes. Other types of leguminous plants yield medicines, dyes and oils.

While many types of beans are cultivated throughout the world, varieties of the kidney bean are the most important in the United States and Canada. Kidney beans were first cultivated by the Indians of South and Central America. Among the many varieties of the kidney bean are the red kidney, the mottled pinto and the white navy. Navy beans became internationally known for their use in Boston baked beans. Kidney beans have a much greater food value than most of the other legumes.

Lima beans are large, flat, white beans that can be eaten dried or green (fresh). Limas are considered to be the most nutritious member of the pea family. The large lima bean often grows to be an inch wide and 1/4 inch thick. High in protein and rich in vitamin B, this bean was first found in the southern areas of the United States. Now it is grown in many have become an important crop in California, where they are planted in May and ripen around September.

Pinto beans are beige-colored and speckled. These beans are popular in stews, chilis, refried beans and other Mexican dishes.

Dry beans are very rich in protein, carbohydrates and fiber and are often eaten as a substitute for meat.

Soups made from dried beans are among the world's oldest culinary dishes. The cultivation of leguminous plants goes back 4,000 years.

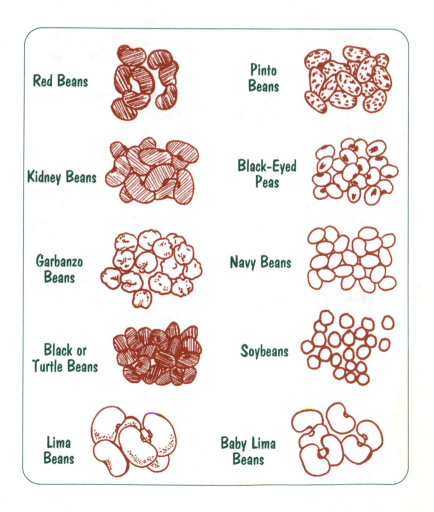

Red Beans

Pinto Beans

Kidney Beans

Black-Eyed Peas

Garbanzo Beans

Navy Beans

Black or Turtle Beans

Soybeans

Lima Beans

Baby Lima Beans

Bean Cooking Tips

Beans are easy to prepare if you know what to do! The following cooking tips are also featured throughout this book. Take a few moments to review them and learn the secrets of creating great bean dishes!

- Tenderness can be tested by the old art of "woofing" the beans. Place a few beans on a saucer and blow across them. If they crack they are tender.

- Add acidic ingredients like tomatoes, tomato sauces, vinegar and lemon juice after the beans have already begun to soften. (Acid slows the cooking process as does the calcium in molasses.)

- Most dried beans take from 2 1/2 - 4 hours to cook. It could take longer if cooking with "hard water" (high in mineral content.) Presoak the beans to reduce this time by an hour.

- Beans can be soaked overnight or several hours prior to cooking. Do not salt soaking water as this will make the skin of the beans tough.

- To de-gas beans, add a 1/2 teaspoon of baking soda to the soaking water. Then use this same water for cooking the beans several hours later or the next day. Another method is to discard the soaking water and add fresh cold water before cooking. Discarding the initial water will help reduce the bean sugar. This sugar seems to be the primary culprit in producing digestive discomfort in some indivduals.

- If you forget to soak your beans, use 6 cups of water per 1 pound of beans. Bring to a boil for 2 minutes, then allow to soak for one hour.

- Adding 2 tablespoons of oil to the cooking water prevents foaming.

- Cooking beans in a crockpot takes from 6 to 8 hours or overnight.

- Always keep beans covered with liquid when cooking to prevent them from drying out and getting tough.

- Store legumes in a cool dry place, (airtight bags or jars).

- Never refrigerate dry beans.

- One cup of cooked or canned beans supplies 12 to 15 grams of vegetable protein, depending on the variety.

- Beans contain no cholesterol unless animal fats are added in cooking to season. They are also naturally low in sodium.

- Beans are an excellent source of dietary fiber, protein, vitamins and minerals. They are also very low in fat.

- Experts note that a cup of cooked dried beans everyday can help control cholesterol, lowering LDL's (low density lipoproteins, the "bad" cholesterol), as well as aid in the control of insulin and blood sugar.

Yields for Legumes

TYPE OF BEANS (1 cup)	YIELD (cups cooked)
Black Beans	4
Black-Eyed Peas	3 1/2
Garbanzos/Chickpeas	4
Great Northern Beans	4
Kidney Beans	4
Lentils	4 1/2
Lima Beans	2 1/2
Limas, Baby	3 1/2
Navy Beans	4
Pink Beans	4
Pinto Beans	4
Red Beans	4
Small White Beans	4
Split Peas	4 1/2

Dried beans, with the exception of lentils and split peas, should be soaked in water before cooking. When cooking, make sure the beans are always covered with liquid. Cooking times can range from 1/2 hour to over 3 hours depending on size and density of beans and cooking procedure used.

Glossary

ANASAZI BEANS®: Versatile, medium-sized red and white beans that are suitable for any bean recipe.

BLACK BEANS: Small black bean with a smoky taste that lends itself to salsas, salads, casseroles, soups and stews.

BLACK-EYED PEAS: Sometimes called "cowpeas," a deep South favorite. Especially good cooked with ham or chicken.

CANNELLINI BEANS: Large white beans that taste similar to green beans when dry. Great in soups.

FAVA BEANS: These were the only beans known in Europe prior to the discovery of the Americas. They can be eaten green or dried. Try them in a cream or tomato sauce.

GARBANZOS: Sometimes referred to as "chickpeas." The nut-like flavor and texture lend the ability to mix with other vegetables.

GREAT NORTHERN BEANS: A larger white bean with a mild taste. Good for making baked beans, soups and salads.

KIDNEY BEANS: Rich maroon color, firm texture and meaty flavor. Great for salads, casseroles and soups.

LENTILS: A variety of colors, these round, flat seeds from the pods of the lentil plant are a great source of protein and fiber.

LIMA BEANS: Referred to as "butter beans" and "the aristocrat of dry beans" because of its large size and buttery flavor. Excellent in casseroles, soups and with smoked meats and cheese.

LIMAS, BABY: Shaped like large limas, but are actually a dry form of fresh green limas. Cooks quickly, mashes easily.

NAVY BEANS: A small white dried bean related to the common kidney bean. It got its name from its use in the U.S. Navy.

PINK BEANS: Fine for chili con carne, BBQ beans or other Mexican-American favorites. Great in soups and stews.

PINTO BEANS: A spotted southwestern favorite. Cooked, mashed and fried again, they have become a Mexican food staple.

RED BEANS: Cousin of the kidney bean. A natural for chili and soups. A colorful addition to three-bean salad.

SMALL WHITE BEANS: This bean is smaller & firmer than the traditional Navy bean, and so it holds its shape better during long, slow cooking and baking.

SOYBEANS: Native to China and India, the bean is a source of oil, flour and a variety of other products.

SPLIT PEAS: A green or yellow pea that has been shelled, dried and split. Used especially in soups.

Appetizers

Black Bean Dip

1 (15 oz.) can BLACK BEANS
2 GARLIC CLOVES
2 Tbsp. LEMON JUICE
1/2 tsp. SALT
4 Tbsp. SALSA

In a food processor or blender, purée all ingredients together. Serve with your favorite chips, crackers or wedges of pita bread.

Creamy Pinto Bean Dip

1 (15 oz.) can REFRIED BEANS
1 (8 oz.) package CREAM CHEESE,
**   (room temperature)**
4 Tbsp. chunky SALSA
1/2 tsp. GARLIC SALT

Blend all of the ingredients thoroughly. Serve with tortilla chips or spread on crisped corn tortillas that have been quartered. These can be heated in a toaster oven or microwave.

Frijole Dip

2 (15 oz.) cans REFRIED BEANS
1 (8 oz.) container SOUR CREAM
1/2 cup SALSA
1/2 tsp. GARLIC POWDER

Blend all ingredients together until creamy. This dip can be served chilled or can be zapped in the microwave on medium temperature for a couple of minutes. If serving warm, try a little shredded cheese on top. Serve with lots of tortilla chips. This is also great with warmed flour tortillas.

Bean salsas are especially good served with chicken, pork and beef dishes.

Black Bean Salsa

A Southwestern favorite!

1 (15 oz.) can BLACK BEANS, drained
1 can (15.25 oz.) CORN, drained
1 Tbsp. OLIVE OIL
2 chopped TOMATOES
4 Tbsp. diced GREEN CHILES
4 sliced GREEN ONIONS
1/2 cup chopped fresh CILANTRO
1/4 tsp. GARLIC SALT
1 Tbsp. LEMON JUICE

Combine all of the ingredients together and refrigerate until well chilled.

Spicy Garbanzo Crunchies

*These snacks are easy to make
and a delicious change
from roasted nuts.*

**1 (15 oz.) can GARBANZO BEANS
1 Tbsp. OIL
1/2 tsp. GARLIC SALT
1/4 tsp. CAYENNE PEPPER
1/4 tsp. CHILI POWDER**

Place thoroughly drained garbanzos in a shallow bowl. Coat with oil and seasonings. Mix well making sure that all of the seasonings are well distributed covering the beans. Spread garbanzos in a single layer on a cookie sheet. Bake in a 350 degree oven for 30 minutes or until garbanzos are crunchy.

Acid slows the cooking process, so always wait to add tomatoes or vinegar until beans are almost done. The calcium in molasses has the same effect.

Bean & Cheese Dip

2 cups REFRIED BEANS
1 cup shredded LONGHORN
    CHEESE
2 chopped GREEN ONIONS
3 Tbsp. SALSA

Mix ingredients together and heat thoroughly. This may be done on the stove top, simmering over low heat and stirring often or microwave on medium, stirring occasionally. Serve hot with chips or warmed flour tortillas.

Pinto beans are a good source of protein and iron. Adding cheese to your dish provides an even better source of protein.

Chunky Bean Dip

1 cup REFRIED BEANS
1/2 cup chopped WALNUTS or PECANS
1 chopped stalk CELERY
2 Tbsp. MAYONNAISE
1/2 tsp. GARLIC SALT

Combine all of the ingredients together and mix well.

Broiled Falafel Patties

*Falafel is a traditional
Middle Eastern food.*

**2 cups cooked GARBANZO BEANS
1/2 cup fresh PARSLEY clusters
1/4 cup BUTTER
2 GARLIC CLOVES
1 EGG, beaten with 1 Tbsp. water
1/2 tsp. DRY MUSTARD
1 tsp. CUMIN
1/2 tsp. CHILI POWDER
1 tsp. WORCESTERSHIRE SAUCE
SALT & PEPPER to taste
OIL as needed**

Preheat oven to 350 degrees. Purée the beans and parsley in a blender or food processor, then put mixture in a mixing bowl and add remaining ingredients except for the oil. Mix thoroughly and spoon by tablespoonful onto an oiled baking sheet. Flatten each patty and brush tops with oil. Bake for about 15 minutes or until crispy and golden, or you can broil for a few minutes on each side.

These are great served with a ranch or Thousand Island type of dressing.

Beanballs

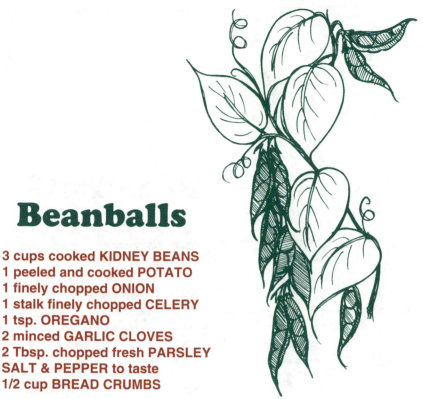

3 cups cooked KIDNEY BEANS
1 peeled and cooked POTATO
1 finely chopped ONION
1 stalk finely chopped CELERY
1 tsp. OREGANO
2 minced GARLIC CLOVES
2 Tbsp. chopped fresh PARSLEY
SALT & PEPPER to taste
1/2 cup BREAD CRUMBS

Mash the beans and potato together with a potato masher. Add the onion, celery and herbs and mix well. Form the mixture into 24 small balls. Roll each ball in the bread crumbs and place on a lightly greased baking sheet. Bake at 350 degrees for 30 minutes. Serve with your favorite dressing, dip or salsa.

Depending on the variety, one cup of cooked or canned beans supplies 12 to 15 grams of vegetable protein.

Bean Paté

1/2 chopped RED ONION
2 GARLIC CLOVES
1 (15 oz.) can WHITE BEANS,
    drained and rinsed
3/4 cup BREAD CRUMBS
1 Tbsp. OLIVE OIL
1 Tbsp. LEMON JUICE
1 tsp. COARSE BROWN MUSTARD
2 Tbsp. PARSLEY
1 Tbsp. chopped fresh BASIL
1/2 tsp. each OREGANO, THYME,
    DILLWEED & TARRAGON
SALT & PEPPER to taste

In a food processor, mince onion and garlic. Add remaining ingredients and process until smooth, stopping once or twice to scrape mixture down the sides of the processor. Taste and adjust seasonings if needed. Cover and refrigerate for at least one hour.

White Beans
- *Great Northern*
- *Navy*
- *Cannelini*

Any Bean Salsa

1 (15 oz.) can drained BEANS,
    (favorite bean of choice)
2 lg. diced TOMATOES
1/4 cup diced ONION
1 diced CUCUMBER
4 Tbsp. diced GREEN CHILES
1/2 cup diced fresh CILANTRO
1/4 tsp. GARLIC SALT
1 Tbsp. LEMON JUICE

Combine all of the ingredients together and chill for one hour.

Lima Snacks

This is a nutritious and delicious snack!

1 (12 oz.) box frozen BABY LIMA BEANS
1 Tbsp. OIL
1/2 tsp. GARLIC SALT

Allow frozen limas to thaw completely on an absorbent towel. In a shallow bowl, toss the lima beans with the oil, coating thoroughly. Spread the coated beans in a single layer on a cookie sheet. Sprinkle with garlic salt and any other seasoning that you favor. Bake in a 350 degree oven for 30 minutes, or until the beans are toasted with a crunchy texture. Serve at room temperature.

Soups

Navy Bean Soup

1 lb. dried NAVY BEANS, soaked
    overnight in 6 cups water
4 cups STOCK or WATER
1 cup chopped ONION
1 minced GARLIC CLOVE
1 cup chopped CELERY
2 Tbsp. OIL or BUTTER
1 cup chopped CARROTS
SALT & PEPPER to taste
chopped fresh PARSLEY

Drain beans. Put beans and stock in a large soup kettle and bring to a boil. Simmer gently on low heat. Meanwhile, sauté onion, garlic and celery in oil until translucent and just beginning to brown. Add to beans. Stir in carrots. Add enough water to cover the beans by 1 inch. Simmer covered for 1 hour, stirring occasionally and adding more water if necessary. (Beans should always be slightly covered with the simmering broth.) Add salt and pepper; cook for another 30 minutes, or until beans are very tender. Garnish with chopped parsley.

Hearty Minestrone

This soup is more like a meal!

2 Tbsp. OLIVE OIL
1 medium ONION, chopped
1 cup chopped CELERY
1 cup chopped CARROTS
1 cup diced POTATOES
1 (16 oz.) can STEWED
        TOMATOES, coarsely chopped
1 (8 oz.) can TOMATO SAUCE
6 cups STOCK or WATER
1 (15 oz.) can KIDNEY BEANS, drained

1 (15 oz.) can GARBANZO
    BEANS, drained
2 cups shredded CABBAGE
1 cup sliced ZUCCHINI
1/2 tsp. dried OREGANO
1/2 tsp. dried THYME

1/2 tsp. dried BASIL
1/2 cup uncooked ELBOW
    MACARONI
SALT & PEPPER to taste
grated PARMESAN
    CHEESE

    Put oil in large soup pot and sauté onions, celery, and carrots until onions become translucent. Add potatoes, tomatoes, tomato sauce and stock; bring to a boil, then turn down heat and simmer uncovered for 45 minutes. Add beans, cabbage, zucchini, seasonings and macaroni. Cook 15 to 20 minutes or until pasta is done. (Add water if necessary). Top with Parmesan cheese.

Legume & Barley Soup

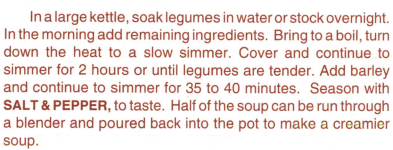

2 cups of LEGUMES*
8 cups WATER or STOCK
1 chopped ONION
2 ribs chopped CELERY
2 sliced CARROTS
1 chopped GARLIC CLOVE
1 BAY LEAF
1 cup uncooked BARLEY

In a large kettle, soak legumes in water or stock overnight. In the morning add remaining ingredients. Bring to a boil, turn down the heat to a slow simmer. Cover and continue to simmer for 2 hours or until legumes are tender. Add barley and continue to simmer for 35 to 40 minutes. Season with **SALT & PEPPER,** to taste. Half of the soup can be run through a blender and poured back into the pot to make a creamier soup.

If you would like a heartier soup, put a **HAM BONE** or chunked **HAM** in the kettle before cooking but after soaking.

* Your favorite or any combination.

A legume is the seed of a vegetable having pods such as peas, lentils, soybeans, black-eyed peas, garbanzos, pintos, limas and many more.

Five Bean Soup

1/3 cup GARBANZO BEANS
1/3 cup KIDNEY BEANS
1/3 cup PINTO BEANS
1/3 cup BLACK-EYED PEAS
1/3 cup GREAT NORTHERN BEANS
6 cups WATER
1 chopped ONION
2 diced CARROTS
2 chopped stalks CELERY
2 minced GARLIC CLOVES
1/2 tsp. OREGANO
SALT & PEPPER to taste
1 BAY LEAF
1 cup chopped HAM

Soak beans overnight. Put drained, soaked beans in a large pot with 6 cups of water and remaining ingredients. Bring to a boil. Reduce heat and cover pot, simmer for 3 1/2 hours or until beans are tender.

Tenderness of cooked beans can be tested by the old art of "woofing" the beans. Place a few beans on a saucer and blow across them. If they crack they are tender.

Black Bean Soup

This soup is delicious served hot or chilled!

2 (15 oz.) cans BLACK BEANS, drained
2 (15 oz.) cans CHICKEN STOCK
1/2 cup chopped ONION
1 chopped CARROT
1 stalk chopped CELERY
SALT & PEPPER to taste
1/2 cup DRY SHERRY
thin slices of LEMON

Combine black beans, chicken stock, onion, carrot and celery in a saucepan. Bring to a boil. Cover and simmer on low heat until vegetables are tender. Add salt and pepper, stir in the sherry. Ladle into bowls and garnish with lemon slices.

To de-gas beans, discard the soaking water and add fresh cold water before cooking. Discarding the initial water will help reduce the bean sugar. This sugar seems to be the primary culprit in producing digestive discomfort in some individuals.

Lentil & Rice Soup

This soup can be frozen and re-heated with excellent results!

1 chopped ONION
2 stalks chopped CELERY
2 chopped CARROTS
2 minced GARLIC CLOVES
2 Tbsp. BUTTER
8 cups WATER
1 lb. LENTILS
2 tsp. SALT
1/4 tsp. PEPPER
1/2 tsp. BASIL
1/2 tsp. OREGANO
1/2 tsp. THYME
1 1/2 cup WATER
1/2 cup RICE

In a large soup kettle, sauté onion, celery, carrots and garlic in butter. When tender, add the 8 cups of water and the lentils. Bring to a boil, reduce heat, cover and simmer gently for about 1 hour. Stir in seasonings and additional 1 1/2 cup water. Cover and continue to simmer for 30 minutes. Add rice and cook another 20 to 30 minutes more or until rice is done. Remove from heat and let cool a bit before serving.

Bean recipes taste even better the second time around. Bean dishes may be kept about 4 or 5 days if refrigerated.

Vegetable Bean Soup

2 cups chopped ONION
1 cup chopped CARROTS
1 cup chopped CELERY
3 Tbsp. BUTTER or MARGARINE
5 cups WATER
3 CHICKEN or BEEF BOUILLON
      CUBES
1 (28 oz.) can TOMATOES,
      coarsely chopped
1 (15 oz.) can PINTO or BLACK
      BEANS, drained
1 (15 oz.) can GREAT NORTHERN
      BEANS, drained
1 tsp. GARLIC POWDER

In a large saucepan, sauté onion, carrots and celery in butter until onion is translucent. Stir in water, bouillon, tomatoes, beans and garlic powder and bring to a boil. Reduce heat and simmer, covered for 15 minutes or until vegetables are tender.

Soups made from dried beans are among the world's oldest culinary dishes. The cultivation of leguminous plants goes back 4,000 years.

Kidney Bean Soup

This hearty soup will warm any appetite

2 Tbsp. BUTTER
1 lg. chopped ONION
2 stalks sliced CELERY
2 sliced CARROTS
2 minced cloves GARLIC
2 (15 oz.) cans KIDNEY BEANS,
    with liquid
4-6 oz. cubed HAM
4 cups WATER
1 Tbsp. WORCESTERSHIRE SAUCE
2 Tbsp. finely chopped, fresh
    PARSLEY
1/2 tsp. ground OREGANO
2 BAY LEAVES
1 Tbsp. LEMON JUICE
SALT & PEPPER to taste

In a large saucepan, melt butter. Add onion and sauté until limp. Add celery, carrot and garlic and continue to sauté for a few minutes until soft. Add kidney beans with liquid, ham and water. Bring to a boil. Cook soup for a couple of minutes then add the Worcestershire sauce, parsley, oregano, bay leaves and lemon juice. Bring to a boil again and cook for about 15 minutes. Season with salt and pepper to taste. Remove bay leaves. Serve piping hot.

Lentil Soup

This quick & easy soup tastes great served with hot, buttered corn bread!

2 cups LENTILS
2 quarts COLD WATER
1 HAM BONE
1 sm. chopped ONION
2 ribs diced CELERY
1 diced CARROT
SALT & PEPPER to taste

Cook lentils in two quarts cold water and the rest of the ingredients for about two hours or until soft. This soup can be put through a sieve; it is also great with the lentils left whole.

Lima Bean Soup

1 cup dried LIMA BEANS
1 quart STOCK or WATER
2 ribs chopped CELERY
2 diced CARROTS
1 chopped ONION
2 Tbsp. BUTTER
1 tsp. SALT

Soak lima beans in 1 quart stock or water overnight. In the morning, add remaining ingredients. Cover and simmer for two to three hours or until tender.

Split Pea Soup

This soup is great on a cold winter day, served with lots of hot crusty bread!

1 lb. dried SPLIT PEAS
1 MEATY HAM BONE (optional)
8 cups WATER
1 chopped ONION
2 stalks chopped CELERY
2 chopped CARROTS
1 diced POTATO
1/2 tsp. OREGANO
1/2 tsp. THYME
3/4 tsp. GARLIC SALT
1/4 tsp. PEPPER

In a large kettle, bring peas, ham bone, water and onion to a boil. Lower heat and simmer, covered, for about 1 hour. Add celery, carrots, potatoes and seasonings. Bring to a boil once again, then reduce heat, cover and simmer for another 30 minutes or until vegetables are very tender. Stir soup occasionally during cooking process to prevent peas from sticking. Add more water if needed for desired consistency.

Split peas are a green or yellow pea that has been shelled, dried and split. They are especially good in soups.

Winter Day Soup

This thick and chunky soup is well worth the wait!

2 cups mixed DRIED BEANS*
2 quarts WATER
2 cups diced HAM or sliced cooked
 SAUSAGES
1 chopped ONION
1 minced GARLIC CLOVE
1 tsp. CHILI POWDER
1 (28 oz.) can TOMATOES
SALT & PEPPER to taste

Rinse beans and place in a large kettle. Cover with water and soak overnight. Drain. Add two quarts fresh water and add meat. Simmer for three hours. Add onion, garlic, chili powder, tomatoes and salt & pepper to taste. Continue simmering for 45 minutes longer. This soup is great served with a crusty bread and a green salad.

*Great Northern, Navy, Pinto, Lima, Black, Garbanzo, Lentils, Split Peas, Black-eyed Peas etc.

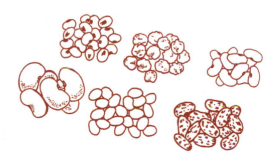

Bean & Split Pea Soup

1/2 cup each, dried:
- **KIDNEY BEANS**
- **NAVY BEANS**
- **PINTO BEANS**
- **BLACK EYED PEAS**

1/2 cup each:
- **YELLOW SPLIT PEAS**
- **GREEN SPLIT PEAS**

9 cups cold WATER or STOCK
3 Tbsp. BUTTER
2 thinly sliced ONIONS
2 thinly sliced CARROTS
4 thinly sliced stalks CELERY
1 crushed clove GARLIC
1 lb. POLISH SAUSAGE (Kielbasa)
1 (28 oz.) can WHOLE TOMATOES
SALT & PEPPER to taste

Wash beans and peas. Soak overnight covered in water. Replace soaking water with fresh water or stock. Bring to a boil, then turn down heat, cover and simmer for an hour or until beans are tender.

While pot is simmering, melt the butter in a large skillet and add onions, carrots, celery and garlic. Cover and cook gently until onions are translucent. Add vegetables to bean and pea mixture. Thinly slice the sausage and brown in the skillet. Remove with a slotted spoon and add to soup pot. Add tomatoes (with liquid), salt and pepper, to taste. Let simmer until ready to serve. Ladle into bowls and serve with bread and a green salad.

Salads

Beans with Pasta & Veggies

8 oz. uncooked ROTELE PASTA
1 cup cooked NAVY BEANS
1 cup cooked KIDNEY BEANS
1 cup cooked BLACK BEANS
1 sliced RED BELL PEPPER
1 cup sliced CARROTS
1 cup BROCCOLI florets
1 cup CAULIFLOWER florets
1/4 cup OLIVE OIL
1/4 cup VINEGAR
1 tsp. SUGAR
1/2 tsp. SALT
1/2 tsp. OREGANO
1/2 tsp. PARSLEY
dash of BLACK PEPPER

Cook pasta according to package directions. Drain and rinse with cold water. Combine all of the ingredients together and chill for at least one hour. Stir gently before serving.

Always keep beans covered with liquid when cooking to prevent them from drying out and getting tough.

Black Bean Salad

1 (15 oz.) can BLACK BEANS,
    drained
3 chopped hard boiled EGGS
1 stalk chopped CELERY
1/3 cup chopped RED ONION
1/2 cup cubed CHEDDAR CHEESE
LETTUCE

Combine all of the ingredients except lettuce. When ready to serve, toss with salad dressing of your choice. Serve on a bed of lettuce.

Mexican Bean Salad

1 (15 oz.) can KIDNEY BEANS, drained
1 (15 oz.) can PINTO BEANS, drained
1 cup SALSA
1 head shredded LETTUCE
1 cup chopped ONION
1 cup chopped TOMATO
1 cup shredded CHEESE
1 lg. bag TORTILLA CHIPS

Combine beans and salsa. Place lettuce on plates and top with bean mixture, onion, tomatoes and cheese. Surround with chips and garnish with **SOUR CREAM** and **SALSA**.

Black-Eyed Pea Salad

Try this deliciously different salad!

2 (15 oz.) cans **BLACK-EYED PEAS,** drained
1 **GREEN BELL PEPPER,** cut into strips
2 stalks diced **CELERY**
1 diced **TOMATO**
1/2 cup chopped **RED ONION**
1/2 tsp. **OREGANO**
1/2 cup **ITALIAN DRESSING**
1 head **LETTUCE,** torn into pieces

Combine all of the ingredients, except for the lettuce and toss gently. Place lettuce in a large salad bowl and spoon bean mixture over lettuce.

Three Bean Salad

2 cups cooked **KIDNEY BEANS**
2 cups cooked **BLACK BEANS**
2 cups cooked **GARBANZO BEANS**
1 thinly sliced **RED ONION**
2 stalks sliced **CELERY**

1 diced **TOMATO**
1/2 cup **OLIVE OIL**
1/4 cup **VINEGAR**
1/2 tsp. **OREGANO**
1Tbsp. **SUGAR**
shredded **LETTUCE**

Combine all of the ingredients, except the lettuce, together in a large bowl. Cover and chill for at least one hour. Serve over shredded lettuce.

Zesty Garbanzo Bean Salad

1 (15 oz.) can GARBANZO BEANS, drained
1/4 cup chopped, fresh PARSLEY
2 Tbsp. CHILI SAUCE
1/2 tsp. OREGANO
1/4 cup ITALIAN DRESSING
CRISP SALAD GREENS

Combine all of the ingredients except for the salad greens. Chill thoroughly. Serve on salad greens.

Store all legumes in a cool dry place, such as airtight bags or jars.

Hearty Bean Salad

1 (15 oz.) can KIDNEY BEANS, drained
1/2 lb. VELVEETA® CHEESE, cubed
4 chopped HARD-BOILED EGGS
2 stalks chopped CELERY
1 sm. RED ONION, sliced into rings
1/2 cup THOUSAND ISLAND DRESSING

Combine all ingredients and chill thoroughly. Serve on a bed of **LETTUCE** leaves.

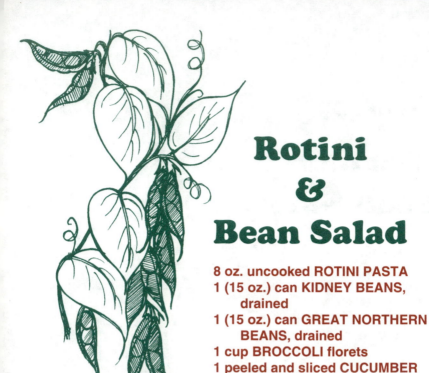

Rotini & Bean Salad

8 oz. uncooked ROTINI PASTA
1 (15 oz.) can KIDNEY BEANS,
**   drained**
1 (15 oz.) can GREAT NORTHERN
**   BEANS, drained**
1 cup BROCCOLI florets
1 peeled and sliced CUCUMBER
1/2 cup chopped RED BELL
**   PEPPER**
1/2 cup sliced BLACK OLIVES
1/2 cup ITALIAN DRESSING

Cook rotini according to package directions. Drain and rinse with cold water. In a large bowl, combine all of the ingredients together. Cover and refrigerate for at least one hour to blend flavors. Toss gently before serving.

There are two types of red kidney beans, light reds and dark reds. Idaho and Washington produce nearly all of the kidney bean crop, with the balance grown all across the country.

Garbanzo & Artichoke Salad

1 lb. cooked **GARBANZO BEANS**
1 sm. jar marinated **ARTICHOKE HEARTS**, drained and sliced
1 sliced **RED BELL PEPPER**
1 sliced **GREEN BELL PEPPER**
1 sliced **RED ONION**
1 peeled and sliced **CUCUMBER**
1 shredded **CARROT**
2 Tbsp. diced **PIMENTO**
1/2 cup sliced **BLACK OLIVES**
2 cups shredded **LETTUCE**
ITALIAN DRESSING

Combine all of the ingredients together. Drizzle with your favorite Italian dressing and toss well.

1 pound of dry beans = 2 cups dry beans
2 cups dry beans = 5 to 6 cups cooked beans

Peppy Pasta & Bean Salad

1/2 lb. ROTINI PASTA
1 RED BELL PEPPER, sliced into
   strips
1/4 cup chopped RED ONION
2 sliced ZUCCHINI
2 minced GARLIC CLOVES
3/4 tsp. ITALIAN SEASONING
1/3 cup and 2 Tbsp. OLIVE OIL
1 (15 oz.) can KIDNEY BEANS
2 Tbsp. minced fresh PARSLEY
juice of 1 LEMON
3/4 tsp. HOT PEPPER SAUCE
SALT & PEPPER to taste

Cook pasta according to package directions, drain. In a large skillet, sauté red bell pepper, onion, zucchini, garlic and Italian seasoning in 2 tablespoons oil until tender but still crisp. Let vegetables cool. In a large bowl, toss pasta, beans and vegetables together. Chill for several hours. Just before serving, whisk together the remaining 1/3 cup of olive oil, parsley, lemon juice, pepper sauce, salt and pepper. Pour over pasta, vegetables and beans; toss to coat thoroughly.

Tuna-Bean Salad

1 (15 oz.) can **KIDNEY BEANS**,
    drained
2 (7 oz.) cans **TUNA**, drained
8 chopped **GREEN ONIONS**
2 minced **GARLIC CLOVES**
1/3 cup **OLIVE OIL**
1/4 cup **VINEGAR**
1/4 cup chopped, fresh **PARSLEY**
SALT & PEPPER to taste
LETTUCE

    In a large bowl, combine all ingredients except lettuce. Toss to blend and serve and serve on lettuce leaves. This salad may be served warm or chilled.

Taco Salad

1 (15 oz.) can **PINTO BEANS**, drained
1 (15 oz.) can **KIDNEY BEANS**, drained
1 lb. cooked ground **BEEF** or **TURKEY**
1 head **LETTUCE**, torn into
    bite-size pieces
1 diced **ONION**
2 chopped **TOMATOES**
1/2 lb. shredded **LONGHORN**
    or **JACK CHEESE**
1 (8 oz.) jar of **SALSA**
1 (4 oz.) can diced **BLACK OLIVES**
TORTILLA CHIPS

    Toss all but the tortilla chips together in a large bowl. Chill. When ready to eat, serve with chips. Additional toppings that go well are **SOUR CREAM** and **AVOCADO**

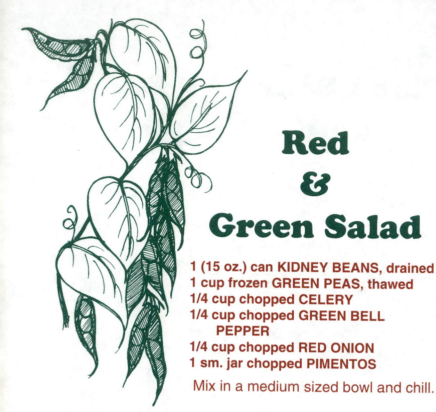

Red & Green Salad

1 (15 oz.) can KIDNEY BEANS, drained
1 cup frozen GREEN PEAS, thawed
1/4 cup chopped CELERY
1/4 cup chopped GREEN BELL
    PEPPER
1/4 cup chopped RED ONION
1 sm. jar chopped PIMENTOS

Mix in a medium sized bowl and chill.

Dressing:

1/2 cup VINEGAR
1/4 cup VEGETABLE OIL

1 tsp. SALT
1/2 cup SUGAR

Mix thoroughly and pour over beans and vegetables. Let sit overnight in the refrigerator. Stir 2 or 3 times. Drain before serving.

This makes a great Christmas salad!

Lentil Salad

1 cup LENTILS
1/2 cup FRENCH DRESSING
SALT & PEPPER to taste
LETTUCE

Cover lentils in water, let cook just below boiling point. When tender, drain and add French dressing and season. Refrigerate for an hour to absorb dressing. Serve on a bed of lettuce.

A variety of colors, these round, flat seeds from the pods of the lentil plant are a great source of protein and fiber.

Garbanzo & Swiss Cheese Salad

2 cups cooked GARBANZO BEANS
1 cup grated SWISS CHEESE
2 cups RED LEAF LETTUCE, torn into pieces
1 bunch SPINACH, torn into pieces
1 cup ICEBURG LETTUCE, torn into pieces
3 diced GREEN ONIONS
1 sliced RED BELL PEPPER
1/2 cup chopped CUCUMBER

Toss all of the ingredients together with your favorite salad dressing. Italian works great!

Navy Bean Salad

2 1/2 cups dried NAVY BEANS
6 cups WATER
2 stalks diced CELERY
1 chopped ONION
1 chopped GREEN BELL PEPPER
1/2 cup VEGETABLE OIL
1/2 cup VINEGAR
1/2 cup SUGAR
1 tsp. DRY MUSTARD
1 crushed GARLIC CLOVE
1/2 tsp. SALT

Rinse and sort through the beans. Place beans in a saucepan covered with water and let stand overnight. Bring the beans to a boil and cook for approximately 2 hours or until tender. Drain and chill.

Combine the remaining ingredients together and mix well. Toss the salad mixture together with the cooked beans. Chill for at least 4 hours before serving. Garnish with TOMATO WEDGES.

Navy beans, also known as Yankee beans, have been served by the U. S. Navy as a staple since the mid-1800's. Navy beans require lengthy, slow cooking.

Sunshine Salad

2 cups cooked GARBANZO BEANS
1 (15.25) can CORN, drained
1 cup sliced CELERY
1/2 cup chopped ONION
1/4 cup diced GREEN BELL PEPPER
1/4 cup diced RED BELL PEPPER

Combine ingredients and moisten to taste with **Golden Sunshine Dressing.** Chill and serve.

Golden Sunshine Dressing

1/3 cup SUGAR
1/2 tsp. DRY MUSTARD
1 tsp. SALT
2 Tbsp. FLOUR
1 EGG
1/2 cup VINEGAR
1/2 cup WATER
1 Tbsp. BUTTER

Mix dry ingredients. Beat egg with fork in a small bowl. Beat in dry mixture. Heat vinegar, water and butter in a saucepan. Remove from heat and gradually add egg mixture, stirring quickly. Then put back on burner to cook, stirring constantly for 2-3 minutes, until smooth and thick.

Makes 1 1/2 cups of dressing.

Summer Bean Salad

1 (15 oz.) can KIDNEY BEANS, drained
1 (15 oz.) can GREAT NORTHERN BEANS, drained
1/2 cup chopped CELERY
1/2 cup chopped ONION
1 diced CUCUMBER
2 shredded CARROTS
3/4 cup MAYONNAISE
1/4 cup VINEGAR
1/2 cup SUGAR
SALT & PEPPER to taste

Combine all of the ingredients together and mix thoroughly. Allow to chill, preferably overnight.

For a heartier salad, add diced, cooked **HAM** and chunks of **CHEESE**.

Zesty Bean Salad

1 (15 oz.) can KIDNEY BEANS, drained
1 (15 oz.) can BLACK BEANS, drained
1 (15 oz.) can PINTO BEANS, drained
1 (4 oz.) can diced GREEN CHILES, drained
4 diced GREEN ONIONS
1 cup shredded CHEDDAR CHEESE
1 Tbsp. crushed RED PEPPERS
1 pint SOUR CREAM

Combine all ingredients in a large bowl. Refrigerate until well chilled.

Calico Bean Salad

1 (15 oz.) can KIDNEY BEANS, drained
1 (15 oz.) can GARBANZO BEANS, drained
1 (15 oz.) can LIMA
1 chopped RED ONION
1 chopped GREEN BELL PEPPER
1/2 cup OIL
1/2 cup VINEGAR
1/2 cup SUGAR
1/2 tsp. GARLIC SALT
1/4 tsp. BLACK PEPPER
1/2 tsp. GROUND OREGANO

Combine all of the ingredients together in a large bowl. Refrigerate for a couple of hours. This salad tastes best when marinated overnight. Stir before serving.

In the South, dried limas are frequently referred to as butter beans. When mottled with purple they're called calico or speckled butter beans.

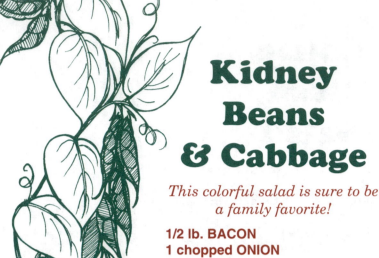

Kidney Beans & Cabbage

This colorful salad is sure to be a family favorite!

1/2 lb. BACON
1 chopped ONION
1 cup MAYONNAISE
1/4 cup VINEGAR
2 Tbsp. SUGAR
3 cups shredded CABBAGE
1 cup diced CELERY
2 (15 oz.) cans KIDNEY BEANS,
    drained

Fry bacon, drain and reserve 1/4 cup of the bacon drippings. Sauté onion in the drippings until limp, remove from the heat. Stir in the mayonnaise, vinegar and sugar. Mix thoroughly. Crumble bacon and add shredded cabbage, celery and beans stirring into the mayonnaise mixture. Serve on crisp **LETTUCE LEAVES** and garnish with **TOMATO WEDGES**.

White Bean Salad

2 (15 oz.) cans GREAT NORTHERN BEANS, drained
1 (4 oz.) jar diced PIMENTOS
2 chopped GREEN ONIONS
1/2 cup FRENCH or ITALIAN DRESSING

Combine all ingredients and chill in refrigerator for at least one hour before serving.

Four Bean Salad

1 (16 oz.) can YELLOW WAX BEANS
1 (16 oz.) can GREEN BEANS
1 (15 oz.) can KIDNEY BEANS
1 (15 oz,) can GARBANZO BEANS
1/4 cup HONEY
1/4 cup CIDER VINEGAR
2 Tbsp. OIL
1 Tbsp. chopped, fresh PARSLEY
1 tsp. ground OREGANO
SALT & PEPPER to taste
4 chopped GREEN ONIONS
1/2 GREEN BELL PEPPER, sliced thin
1/2 RED ONION, sliced into thin rings

Combine all beans in a colander and drain well. In a small bowl, whisk together the honey, vinegar, oil, parsley, salt, pepper and oregano until smooth. In a large bowl, combine remaining ingredients. Toss together with dressing. Allow to marinate in the refrigerator for at least 30 minutes and stir before serving.

Beans can be soaked overnight or several hours prior to cooking. Do not salt soaking water as this will make the skin of the beans tough.

Main Dishes

Beans & Burger

1 lb. lean GROUND BEEF
1 chopped ONION
2 cups cooked KIDNEY BEANS
2 cups cooked PINTO BEANS
2 cups cooked NAVY BEANS
2 tsp. WORCESTERSHIRE SAUCE
4 Tbsp. KETCHUP
2 tsp. PREPARED MUSTARD
2 Tbsp. BROWN SUGAR
1 tsp. CHILI POWDER
1 tsp. GARLIC SALT
1/4 tsp. PEPPER
1/4 tsp. ground OREGANO

In a large skillet or Dutch oven, cook ground beef and onions over medium heat until the meat is browned and the onions are translucent. Drain and add all of the remaining ingredients. Mix thoroughly, cover and simmer on low heat, stirring occasionally for approximately 20 minutes or until heated completely.

Experts note that a cup of cooked dried beans everyday can help control cholesterol, lowering LDL's (low density lipoproteins, the "bad" cholesterol), as well as aid in the control of insulin and blood sugar.

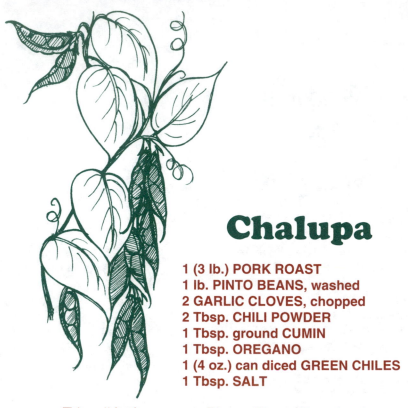

Chalupa

1 (3 lb.) PORK ROAST
1 lb. PINTO BEANS, washed
2 GARLIC CLOVES, chopped
2 Tbsp. CHILI POWDER
1 Tbsp. ground CUMIN
1 Tbsp. OREGANO
1 (4 oz.) can diced GREEN CHILES
1 Tbsp. SALT

Trim all fat from roast. Place all ingredients in a large pot, kettle, or crock pot and cover with water. Simmer over low heat, adding water if needed. After 6 hours, remove bones and break up roast. Continue cooking with lid off until thick. Serve on tostada shells with chopped lettuce, onion, tomatoes, avocado and cheese. Or, roll up a generous amount in a large warm flour tortilla, like a burro. Chalupa freezes perfectly!

This chunky combination makes great tostadas and burros. Ole!

Black-Eyed Pea Casserole

1 1/2 lbs. GROUND ROUND
1 lg. chopped ONION
2 minced GARLIC CLOVES
1 (15 oz.) can BLACK-EYED PEAS,
    drained
1 (15 oz.) can STEWED TOMATOES
1 can CREAM OF MUSHROOM SOUP
1 can CREAM OF CHICKEN SOUP
1 dozen CORN TORTILLAS, cut
    into wedges
2 cups shredded CHEDDAR CHEESE

In a skillet, fry ground round, onion and garlic until browned. Drain. Add black-eyed peas, tomatoes and both soups. Layer meat mixture, cheese and tortillas in a greased casserole dish. Topping off with the shredded cheese. Bake in a preheated 350 degree oven for 30 minutes or until bubbly.

This casserole can be made with **GROUND TURKEY** *and substitute any of your favorite* **LEGUMES** *in place of the black-eyed peas.*

Beans & Bow Ties

8 oz. BOW TIE PASTA
2 Tbsp. BUTTER
1 chopped ONION
1 chopped GREEN BELL PEPPER
1 (15 oz.) can KIDNEY BEANS,
    drained
1 (15 oz.) can GREAT NORTHERN
    BEANS, drained
1/2 tsp. OREGANO
1/2 tsp. GARLIC SALT
1/4 tsp. PEPPER

Cook pasta according to package directions. Drain and rinse with cool water. In a skillet, melt butter and sauté onion until it becomes translucent. Add green pepper and sauté 2 minutes. Add beans, pasta and seasonings. Simmer on low, heat thoroughly and serve warm.

For a heartier meal, add **GROUND BEEF, TURKEY** *or any* **LEFTOVER MEATS.**

Easy Chili

1 lb. lean GROUND BEEF
1 (15 oz.) can PINTO BEANS,
    drained
1 chopped ONION
1 (15 oz.) can chopped STEWED
    TOMATOES
1 minced GARLIC CLOVE
2 Tbsp. CHILI POWDER
1 tsp. ground CUMIN
1/4 tsp. ground ALLSPICE

Brown ground beef, drain any excess fat. Add remaining ingredients and simmer together for 20-30 minutes.

Steak Roll-ups

4 MINUTE STEAKS
1 (15 oz.) can REFRIED BEANS
1/4 cup chopped ONIONS
1/2 cup BARBECUE SAUCE

Combine beans, onions, and barbecue sauce in a bowl. Place equal amounts of bean mixture on steaks, roll up and secure with wooden toothpicks or skewers. Brush with more barbecue sauce. Broil for a few minutes, turn and continue cooking until steaks are done.

Stuffed Bell Peppers

1 (15 oz.) can NAVY BEANS, drained
2 Tbsp. OIL
1 chopped ONION
1 cup chopped CELERY
1 can CREAM OF MUSHROOM SOUP
1 (12 oz.) can CORN, drained
1 cup cooked RICE
6 GREEN BELL PEPPERS, seeded
and membranes removed
1 cup shredded JACK or CHEDDAR
CHEESE

Preheat oven to 400 degrees. Mash beans. Heat oil in a skillet and sauté onion and celery. Stir in soup, corn, rice and mashed beans. Fill peppers with stuffing and top with cheese. Place stuffed peppers in a pan, adding an inch of water to keep peppers from burning or drying out. Bake for 1/2 hour, replenishing water in pan if necessary.

If you forget to soak your beans, use 6 cups of water per 1 pound of beans. Bring to a boil for 2 minutes, then allow to soak for one hour. Adding 2 tablespoons of oil to the cooking water prevents foaming.

Bean & Lentil Stew

1 cup dried **LENTILS**
1 (15 oz.) can **GARBANZO BEANS,**
    undrained
2 cups cubed **POTATOES**
1 cup sliced **CARROTS**
2 stalks sliced **CELERY**
1 chopped **ONION**
1 chopped **GREEN BELL PEPPER**
1 (28 oz.) can **STEWED TOMATOES,**
    cut up
1/2 tsp. **OREGANO**
1 tsp. **GARLIC SALT**
1/4 tsp. **PEPPER**

Rinse and drain lentils. In a large saucepan or Dutch oven, combine all of the ingredients and mix well. Bring to a boil. Reduce heat, cover and simmer for 45 minutes to an hour or until vegetables and lentils are tender.

Add acidic ingredients like tomatoes, tomato sauces, vinegar and lemon juice after the legumes have already begun to soften. Even though lentils and split peas do not require soaking, natural acid will keep all legumes from softening properly.

Bean & Beef Casserole

1/2 lb. sliced BACON, diced
1 lb. lean GROUND BEEF
1 chopped ONION
1 (15 oz.) can KIDNEY BEANS
1 (15 oz.) can LIMA BEANS
1 (16 oz.) can PORK AND BEANS
1/2 cup BARBECUE SAUCE
1/2 cup KETCHUP
2 Tbsp. MUSTARD
2 Tbsp. WORCESTERSHIRE SAUCE
3/4 cup packed BROWN SUGAR
3 Tbsp. MOLASSES
1/2 tsp. GARLIC SALT
1/2 tsp. CHILI POWDER

Rinse and drain kidney and lima beans thoroughly. Fry bacon, beef and onion until meat is browned and onion is translucent. Drain. In a greased casserole dish combine meat and onion mixture with all of the beans. In a separate bowl, blend the remaining ingredients together. Stir this sauce into the bean and beef mixture. Cover and bake for 45 minutes in a 350 degree oven. Remove cover and bake an additional 15 minutes.

Any variety of beans may be used, try **BLACK BEANS** *or* **GARBANZO BEANS** *for a distinctively different taste.*

Refried Anasazi Beans®

1 lb. dried ANASAZI BEANS®
6 cups WATER
1/4 cup finely chopped ONION
1 clove GARLIC, crushed
6 slices chopped BACON
1/4 cup chopped GREEN BELL
    PEPPER
1 tsp. CHILI POWDER

In a saucepan, combine beans and water and cook at a gentle boil for 1 1/2 hours or until tender. Drain beans, reserving liquid. In a skillet, sauté onion, pepper, garlic and bacon. Add sautéed ingredients to beans and mash all together, adding liquid a little at a time, until mixture is smooth in consistancy. Serve with tortillas or cornbread.

Note: These refried beans may be frozen for later use.

Anasazi Beans® do not need pre-soaking, cook faster, and are much sweeter than any other bean.

Spicy Turkey & Beans

1 lb. GROUND TURKEY
1 lg. chopped ONION
2 minced GARLIC CLOVES
1 Tbsp. VEGETABLE OIL
1 tsp. GROUND CUMIN
1/2 tsp. each SALT and PEPPER
1 (28 oz.) can cut up WHOLE TOMATOES
1 (15 oz.) can TOMATO SAUCE
1 (15 oz.) can KIDNEY BEANS, drained
1 (15 oz.) can GREAT NORTHERN
        BEANS, drained

In a large saucepan cook turkey, onion and garlic in hot oil over medium heat until turkey is no longer pink and onion is translucent. Drain off any excess fat. Add cumin, salt and pepper. Stir and cook for a minute more. Stir in undrained tomatoes, tomato sauce and beans. Bring to a boil. Reduce heat, cover and simmer for 20 minutes, stirring occasionally. Ladle into serving bowls and garnish with **SOUR CREAM, SHREDDED CHEESE** and chopped **GREEN ONION**.

Beans are an excellent source of dietary fiber, protein, vitamins and minerals. They are also very low in fat.

Chicken with Black Beans

4 half cooked CHICKEN BREASTS
2 cups cooked BLACK BEANS
1/2 cup SALSA
1/2 cup WHITE WINE
1/4 tsp. GARLIC POWDER
SALT & PEPPER to taste

Place chicken breasts on dinner plates. In a bowl, combine beans, salsa, wine and garlic powder. Top each chicken serving with the bean mixture. Season to taste. Heat in microwave on medium-high setting until thoroughly cooked. Serve hot.

Hearty Bean Pie

1 lb. GROUND BEEF or TURKEY
1 Tbsp. WORCESTERSHIRE SAUCE
1/2 tsp. SEASONING SALT
1 (16 oz.) can PORK & BEANS
1 (16 oz.) can TOMATOES
1/4 lb. BACON
1/2 cup BROWN SUGAR

Brown meat and drain off the fat. Add Worcestershire sauce and seasoning salt. Spoon mixture into bottom of a 9 inch pie pan. Mix beans and tomatoes and spoon over meat. Lay bacon strips on top of bean mixture and sprinkle on brown sugar. Bake at 350 degrees for 45 minutes.

Beans & Kielbasa

1 lb. SMOKED KIELBASA SAUSAGE
1 chopped ONION
2 minced GARLIC CLOVES
3 ribs sliced CELERY
2 (15 oz.) cans GREAT NORTHERN
    BEANS, drained
1 (15 oz.) can KIDNEY BEANS, drained
1 (15 oz.) can STEWED TOMATOES
1/2 tsp. OREGANO
1/2 tsp. THYME
1/2 tsp. ROSEMARY
1 Tbsp. BROWN SUGAR

Brown sausage in a large saucepan or Dutch oven. Remove sausage and set aside, reserving 1 teaspoon of the drippings. Add onion, garlic and celery to the drippings and cook until tender-crisp. Add sausage and the rest of the ingredients. Bring to a boil. Lower heat, cover and simmer for 15 minutes. This dish is great served with a green salad and slices of crusty bread.

Dry beans offer the body fuel in the form of carbohydrates to stoke the human engine. Since they digest slowly, they help to satisfy hunger over a long period of time. In addition they help the body use fat efficiently, thus making the most of the protein that they offer.

Quick & Easy Chili

2 lbs. crumbled GROUND BEEF
1 chopped ONION
1 chopped BELL PEPPER
1 (15 oz.) can KIDNEY BEANS, drained
1 (8 oz.) can TOMATO SAUCE
1 (29 oz.) can chopped TOMATOES
1 tsp. GARLIC SALT
2-3 Tbsp. CHILI POWDER
1/8 tsp. CAYENNE PEPPER

Brown ground beef in a glass baking dish in microwave for 6-7 minutes on HIGH, stirring twice. Drain off any excess fat. Cook onion and bell pepper in 2 tablespoons of water in a microproof bowl for 2 minutes on HIGH. Combine with meat and remaining ingredients, mixing thoroughly. Microwave on HIGH for 12 minutes, stirring once. Let stand covered for 5 minutes before serving. Garnish with a dollop of **SOUR CREAM** and shredded **CHEDDAR CHEESE.**

Beans contain no cholesterol unless animal fats are added in cooking for seasoning. They are also naturally low in sodium.

Black Beans & Brown Rice Burritos

1 (15 oz.) can BLACK BEANS, drained
1 finely grated, large ONION
1 (4 oz.) can diced GREEN CHILES
2 Tbsp. chopped fresh CILANTRO
1 tsp. RED CHILI POWDER
8 WHOLE WHEAT FLOUR TORTILLAS
2 cups cooked BROWN RICE
SALT & PEPPER to taste
1 cup SALSA

Preheat oven to 350 degrees. In a large mixing bowl, mash beans with grated onion. Stir in the chiles, cilantro and chili powder. Spread tortillas out on a counter and place equal amounts of the bean mixture on each. Top each with 1/4 cup of cooked brown rice. Fold in sides and roll tortilla to completely enclose contents. Place all eight burritos, seam side down, in a non-stick baking pan. Pour salsa evenly over the burritos and bake at 350 degrees for 20 minutes.

Garnish with **SHREDDED CHEESE, SOUR CREAM** and/or **GUACAMOLE.**

Midwestern Bean Bake

OIL for sautéing
1 chopped ONION
2 EGGS
2 cups MILK
2 Tbsp. DIJON MUSTARD
1 cup shredded CHEDDAR CHEESE
1 cup NAVY BEANS, canned or
      cooked
1 cup KIDNEY BEANS, canned or
      cooked
2 cups cooked RICE
SALT & PEPPER to taste
1 cup chopped TOMATOES
1/2 cup grated JACK or CHEDDAR
      CHEESE

Preheat oven to 350 degrees. Heat oil and sauté onions until they are translucent. Beat eggs in a bowl and add milk, mustard, shredded cheddar cheese, beans, rice and sautéed onion. Season to taste. Spread mixture into an oiled casserole dish. Sprinkle the top with the tomatoes and grated cheese. Bake for about 45 minutes or until it is firm in the middle and brown on top.

The word "protein" comes from a Greek word meaning "to take first place".

Vermont Baked Beans

1 lb. NAVY BEANS
2 Tbsp. OIL
1 1/2 lbs. COUNTRY-STYLE
PORK RIBS
1 lg. chopped ONION
1/3 cup MAPLE SYRUP
1/4 cup BROWN SUGAR
1 1/2 cups WATER
SALT & PEPPER to taste

Soak beans overnight. Preheat oven to 300 degrees. Heat oil in a large skillet and brown pork ribs on all sides. Remove from skillet and place on a platter. Add onion to pan and continue to sauté for five minutes. Stir in maple syrup, sugar and water. Combine with drained, soaked beans and transfer to a large buttered bean pot or Dutch oven. Place pork ribs on beans. Cover and bake for 3 hours or until beans are tender. If too moist, remove ribs and bake uncovered for an additional 10-15 minutes. Season to taste.

Some historians claim that early American Indians flavored their beans with maple sugar while others say sweeteners such as maple sugar and molasses weren't introduced until the middle of the nineteenth century.

Black Bean Chili

1 lb. GROUND BEEF
2 Tbsp. OIL
1 chopped ONION
1 chopped BELL PEPPER
2 crushed GARLIC CLOVES
1 lb. BLACK BEANS, soaked, cooked
    and drained
2 Tbsp. hot CHILI POWDER
1 tsp. CUMIN
1 Tbsp. WORCESTERSHIRE SAUCE
1 (28 oz.) can TOMATOES, cut up
SALT & PEPPER to taste

Brown ground beef in oil along with onion, bell pepper and garlic. Drain excess fat and add all of the remaining ingredients. Simmer for at least 1 1/2 hours or until beans are tender.

Kraut & Beans

1 lg. chopped ONION
6 slices chopped BACON
2 (15 oz.) cans KIDNEY BEANS, drained
1 qt. SAUERKRAUT, drained

Sauté onion and bacon. Add beans and sauerkraut when bacon is crisp. Simmer until thoroughly warmed. Serve hot.

Spicy Vegetable Chili

1 1/2 cups sliced ONIONS
1 1/2 cups sliced CELERY
1 1/2 cups sliced GREEN BELL
    PEPPER
4 cloves minced GARLIC
2 Tbsp. BUTTER
2 (28 oz.) cans chopped WHOLE
    TOMATOES (reserve juice)
3 (15 oz.) cans KIDNEY BEANS
1 (15 oz.) can GREAT NORTHERN
    BEANS
1 Tbsp. CHILI POWDER
1 Tbsp. chopped PARSLEY
2 tsp. SALT
1 tsp. BASIL
1 tsp. OREGANO
1/2 tsp. PEPPER
1/4 tsp. TABASCO® SAUCE
1/4 cup VINEGAR
2 cups shredded CHEDDAR CHEESE

Sauté onion, celery, green pepper and garlic in butter until tender. Stir in tomatoes, tomato juice, and the undrained kidney and great northern beans. Add remaining ingredients, except cheese. Bring to a boil, reduce heat and cover. Simmer for 1 hour. Remove cover and simmer 1 hour longer. Ladle into serving dishes and top with 1/4 cup shredded cheese.

Bean "Burgers"

*This makes a great vegetarian
alternative to hamburgers!*

**3 cups cooked KIDNEY or PINTO
  BEANS**
1 finely chopped ONION
1 cooked POTATO
2 chopped TOMATOES
1 minced clove GARLIC
1 tsp. OREGANO
1 tsp. THYME
3/4 cup BREADCRUMBS
SALT & PEPPER to taste

Mix all ingredients thoroughly, either in a food processor or with potato masher. If mixture is too moist, add more breadcrumbs. Form into eight burgers and place them on a lightly greased baking tray. Bake at 350 degrees for 30 minutes, turn and cook an additional 15 minutes. Serve on hamburger buns with onions, lettuce, tomatoes, pickles and your favorite condiments.

*Black beans or Navy
beans can be substituted for
the pinto beans.*

Tostadas

OIL for frying
5 cups cooked or canned PINTO BEANS
SALT to taste
1 dozen CORN TORTILLAS

Garnishes:
    shredded JACK or CHEDDAR CHEESE
    shredded LETTUCE
    chopped TOMATOES
    chopped ONION
    SALSA
    SOUR CREAM
    BLACK OLIVES
    AVOCADO CHUNKS

In a deep, heavy skillet, heat enough oil to cover bottom of pan. Oil should be very hot but not smoking. Add the beans and, using a wooden spoon, mash the beans against the skillet. The oil should be hot enough to fry the beans. Salt to taste. Fry tortillas briefly in a little bit of oil, or crisp in a hot oven. To assemble: Spread a generous amount of refried beans on each tortilla. Add garnishes, putting the cheese on top of the hot beans to melt.

One tostada includes each of the basic four food groups: Beans and cheese for protein and calcium. The tortilla shell supplies B vitamins, and the lettuce, tomatoes and chile provide vitamins A and C.

Side Dishes

Hoppin' John Peas

This dish is traditionally made with red beans. The black-eyed peas add a distinctively different flavor.

2 cups dried BLACK-EYED PEAS
1 meaty HAM BONE
1 chopped ONION
1 minced GARLIC CLOVE
1 tsp. SALT
1/4 tsp. PEPPER
1 cup INSTANT RICE
1 (16 oz.) can STEWED TOMATOES

Cover black-eyed peas with water and bring to a boil. Add ham bone, onion, garlic, salt and pepper. Cover and simmer for 1 hour and 30 minutes. Remove ham bone. Pour rice on top of the black-eyed peas and add enough water just to cover the rice. Bring to a boil, cover and remove from heat. Let stand covered for 15 minutes to allow the rice to cook. Stir in the tomatoes, warm, and serve.

"Beans are worth their weight in protein", says a recent release from the USDA. A cup of cooked or canned beans supplies about 12 to 15 grams of vegetable protein, depending on variety.

Sweet & Tangy Beans

1 (16 oz.) can PORK & BEANS
1 (28 oz.) can BAKED BEANS with
    bacon and brown sugar
1 (23 oz.) can RANCH STYLE® BEANS
1 (4 oz.) can chopped GREEN CHILES
1 large, chopped ONION
3 large stalks chopped CELERY
1 chopped CARROT
1/4 cup BROWN SUGAR
2 + Tbsp. MOLASSES
1/4 cup BARBECUE SAUCE

    Put all ingredients into a crock pot on LOW. Let simmer all day. If too much liquid remains at the end of cooking time, put in a large saucepan on stove and cook uncovered until desired thickness. Serve with rice.

Cowboy Beans

2 (16 oz.) cans PORK & BEANS
1/2 cup chopped ONION
1 tsp. finely chopped JALAPEÑO
    PEPPER (optional)
1 cup KETCHUP
1/2 cup BROWN SUGAR
2 Tbsp. WORCESTERSHIRE SAUCE
1 Tbsp. PREPARED MUSTARD
2 strips BACON

    Mix all ingredients together except for bacon. Pour into a 2 quart casserole dish. Top with bacon. Bake at 350 degrees for 1 hour. Remove bacon and crumble on top. Stir before serving.

Red Beans

2 cups dried RED BEANS
1/4 cup SALSA
1/2 cup TOMATO PURÉE
1/2 tsp. CHILI POWDER
1/2 tsp. GROUND CUMIN
1 tsp. SALT
dash of DRY MUSTARD

After soaking, wash beans and drain. Place beans in cooking pot with enough water to cover at least 4 inches above the beans. Simmer over medium-low heat for two hours or until tender, add more water if needed. Do not boil rapidly, as skins will burst. Add remaining ingredients and simmer 20 minutes more.

The bush-type plants of small red beans have smooth-bordered, heart-shaped leaves and white, yellow or purple flowers.

New Orleans Red Beans

This dish is great served over steamed rice with lots of cajun sauce on the side.

1 lb. dried RED BEANS
1 chopped ONION
1 chopped GARLIC CLOVE
2 stalks chopped CELERY
1 chopped RED BELL PEPPER
1/2 cup TOMATO PASTE
3 Tbsp. SOY SAUCE

1/2 tsp. each:
  dried OREGANO
  ground CUMIN
  BLACK PEPPER
  PAPRIKA
1/4 tsp. CAYENNE
SALT to taste

Soak beans overnight. Drain and cover with fresh water. Bring to a boil, reduce heat and simmer for 1 1/2 hours. Add remaining ingredients and continue cooking for one hour.

Tangy Black-Eyed Peas

2 cups BLACK-EYED PEAS
1 chopped RED ONION
1 minced GARLIC CLOVE
1 tsp. WORCESTERSHIRE
    SAUCE
2 Tbsp. BUTTER
SALT & PEPPER to taste

Cover peas with water and add onion and garlic. Bring to a boil, reduce heat to a simmer. Cover and cook for 1 hour or until peas are tender. Add remaining ingredients and cook, uncovered, on low heat for another 15 minutes.

Black-Eyed Peas & Ham Hocks

A traditional "Good Luck" dish for the New Year!

2 cups dried BLACK-EYED
    PEAS
4 SMOKED HAM HOCKS
2 stalks chopped CELERY
1 chopped ONION
1 Tbsp. crushed RED PEPPER

2 BAY LEAVES
1 tsp. GARLIC SALT
1/2 tsp. SUGAR
1 tsp. DRY MUSTARD
SALT & PEPPER to taste

Soak peas overnight. Place ham hocks in a large pot and add enough water to cover. Bring to a boil, reduce heat and simmer for 30 minutes. Add black-eyed peas and all of the other ingredients. Simmer until peas are tender and the liquid is almost absorbed. Serve with hot corn bread.

Black-Eyed Peas & Brown Rice

3 cups cooked BLACK-EYED PEAS
1 cup cooked BROWN RICE
1 cup cooked diced MEAT
2 cups CHICKEN STOCK
2 Tbsp. chopped PARSLEY
SALT and PEPPER to taste

Combine cooked peas and rice with other ingredients, heat thoroughly and serve.

Black-eyed peas are also known as "cowpeas".

Chile-Peas

Try this zesty Southwestern dish!

4 cups cooked BLACK-EYED PEAS
1 (4 oz.) can diced GREEN CHILES
4 sliced GREEN ONIONS
1 (15 oz.) can STEWED TOMATOES, drained and chopped
1 minced GARLIC CLOVE
1/4 tsp. ground OREGANO
1/4 tsp. each SALT & PEPPER

Combine all ingredients in a bowl. This dish can be served hot or chilled. If serving cold, add 2 tsp. each of **OIL & VINEGAR**, and refrigerate for 2-3 hours. If serving as a hot dish, simmer on low heat until thoroughly warmed or cover and microwave on medium for 5 minutes.

Mexicali Chickpeas

1 GREEN BELL PEPPER
1 RED BELL PEPPER
1 lb. cooked CHICKPEAS
    or 2 (15 oz.) cans, well drained
1 thinly sliced RED ONION
1/4 cup sliced BLACK OLIVES
1 (4 oz.) can diced GREEN CHILES

Dressing:
  1 minced GARLIC CLOVE
  3 Tbsp. OLIVE OIL
  4 Tbsp. VINEGAR
  1/2 tsp. SALT
  1/4 tsp. BLACK PEPPER
  1/2 tsp. crushed OREGANO

    Coarsely chop the bell peppers, then toss with the next 4 ingredients in a large bowl. In a jar, combine the dressing ingredients; cover and shake vigorously until thoroughly mixed. Drizzle dressing over chickpeas and vegetables. Toss well.

Creamy-yellow garbanzos, often referred to as "chickpeas", are a favorite of Spain and Portugal. Their nut-like flavor mixes well with other vegetables to create fabulous salads and appetizers.

Lima Supreme

2 lb. dried LIMA BEANS
1/2 lb. chopped BACON
1 finely chopped ONION
2 (8 oz.) cans TOMATO PASTE
1 Tbsp. DRY MUSTARD
SALT & PEPPER to taste
1/2 lb. BROWN SUGAR

Soak beans overnight. Cook beans, bacon and onion for 45 minutes to 1 hour. Beans will be firm. Transfer to a large roaster. Add tomato paste, mustard, salt and pepper. Cover and bake at 300 degrees for 1 hour. Remove lid, add sugar and brown slowly, stirring and adding water until well browned, about 4 hours or until desired consistancy.

Baby limas are actually the dry form of fresh green limas. They can be used in most recipes calling for "white beans."

Baked Lima Beans

2 cups dried BABY LIMA BEANS, cooked
1/4 cup BUTTER
1/2 cup BROWN SUGAR
2 Tbsp. KETCHUP
1 Tbsp. MUSTARD
1/2 cup HEAVY CREAM

Combine first 5 ingredients. Fold in cream. Put in a greased 2 quart casserole dish. Bake, uncovered, at 350 degrees for 45 minutes.

Black Bean Relish

2 (15 oz.) cans BLACK BEANS, drained
1 med. RED ONION, diced
1 diced TOMATO
1 chopped BELL PEPPER
1 Tbsp. SALAD OIL
1 Tbsp. VINEGAR
1/2 tsp. GROUND OREGANO
1/2 tsp. GARLIC SALT

Combine all of the ingredients together and mix well. Cover and chill for 1 hour.

Legumes provide protein, calcium, phosphorus, vitamins and other nutrients that are vital for good health.

Black Beans & Rice

2 (15 oz.) cans BLACK BEANS, drained
2 cups cold cooked RICE
1 chopped stalk CELERY
1 sliced GREEN ONION
1 med. chopped TOMATO
1/4 cup OLIVE OIL
1/4 cup LEMON JUICE
1 minced GARLIC CLOVE
1/2 tsp. SALT
1/8 tsp. BLACK PEPPER
1/8 tsp. TABASCO® SAUCE

In a large bowl, combine beans, rice, celery, green onion and tomato; mix well. In a small bowl, whisk remaining ingredients together and fold into beans, rice and vegetable mixture. Cover and refrigerate 1 hour to blend flavors.

Charro Beans

1/2 lb. PINTO or PINK BEANS
1/2 chopped ONION
2 minced GARLIC CLOVES
6 cups WATER
1 JALAPEÑO or ANAHEIM CHILE PEPPER
1/2 lb. lean cooked HAM, cubed
1 cup SALSA
SALT & PEPPER to taste

Combine beans, onion, garlic and water in a large pot and bring to a boil. Lower heat, cover pot and let the beans simmer for about 2 hours or until tender. Cut slits in the sides of the jalapeño pepper and add it and the other remaining ingredients to the beans. Cook uncovered for another 20 minutes over low heat.

Indiana Baked Beans

1 lb. GREAT NORTHERN BEANS
2 cups BROWN SUGAR
1 chopped ONION
1 (28 oz.) bottle KETCHUP
4 slices BACON
SALT & PEPPER to taste

Soak beans overnight. Drain and add fresh water to cover beans completely. Bring to a boil. Reduce heat, cover pot and simmer for about 1 1/2 hours. Place 1/2 of the beans in a large casserole dish. Layer with 1/2 of the brown sugar, 1/2 of the onion and 1/2 of the ketchup. Repeat layer of remaining beans plus all liquid, brown sugar, onion and ketchup. Lay bacon slices on top. Cover and bake in a 300 degree oven for 6 hours. Check occasionally and add hot water if beans become dry.

Barbecued Lima Beans

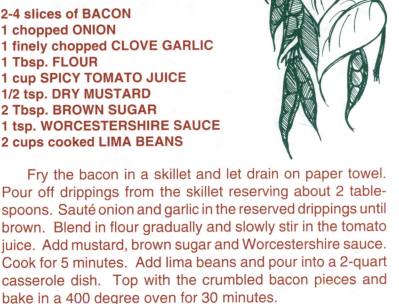

2-4 slices of BACON
1 chopped ONION
1 finely chopped CLOVE GARLIC
1 Tbsp. FLOUR
1 cup SPICY TOMATO JUICE
1/2 tsp. DRY MUSTARD
2 Tbsp. BROWN SUGAR
1 tsp. WORCESTERSHIRE SAUCE
2 cups cooked LIMA BEANS

Fry the bacon in a skillet and let drain on paper towel. Pour off drippings from the skillet reserving about 2 tablespoons. Sauté onion and garlic in the reserved drippings until brown. Blend in flour gradually and slowly stir in the tomato juice. Add mustard, brown sugar and Worcestershire sauce. Cook for 5 minutes. Add lima beans and pour into a 2-quart casserole dish. Top with the crumbled bacon pieces and bake in a 400 degree oven for 30 minutes.

In the South, dried limas are frequently referred to as butter beans. When mottled with purple, they're called calico or speckled butter beans.

Bean-Stuffed Potatoes

2 Tbsp. BUTTER
1/2 tsp. GARLIC SALT
2 sliced GREEN ONIONS
1 stalk CELERY, finely diced
1 (15 oz.) can drained or 2 cups
    cooked PINTO BEANS
4 large hot BAKED POTATOES
1/2 cup shredded CHEDDAR CHEESE
SOUR CREAM

In a saucepan, heat butter until melted. Add garlic salt, green onions and celery. Sauté for about 2 minutes. Stir in beans and heat thoroughly. Split potatoes lengthwise and using a fork, fluff the potatoes. Spoon equal amounts of the bean mixture over the potatoes. Top with shredded cheese and a dollop of sour cream.

Acid slows the cooking process, so always wait to add tomatoes or vinegar until beans are almost done. The calcium in molasses has the same effect.

Fava Beans

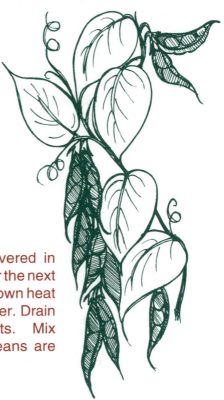

2 cups dried FAVA BEANS
1 chopped ONION
2 minced GARLIC CLOVES
2 chopped TOMATOES
juice of 1 LEMON
2 Tbsp. OLIVE OIL
1/2 tsp. OREGANO
SALT & PEPPER to taste

Soak beans overnight covered in water. Replace with fresh water the next day. Bring to a boil, then turn down heat and simmer until beans are tender. Drain and add remaining ingredients. Mix thoroughly until half of the beans are broken.

Chilibeans

Cover **one pound (2 cups) DRIED PINK BEANS or KIDNEY BEANS** with boiling water and let stand for an hour or so. Drain beans and put into a large, heavy pot, cover with boiling water again and add:

1 chopped ONION
2-3 minced GARLIC CLOVES
1/3 cup BACON DRIPPINGS or COOKING OIL
1 1/2 tsp. SALT
1 (8 oz.) can TOMATO SAUCE
1 1/2 tsp. CHILI POWDER
1/4 tsp. CUMIN

Cover and cook slowly for about three hours, until beans are tender and a rich sauce has formed. Add more hot water if necessary. Beans should be neither too dry nor too juicy.

Luau Beans

4 cups cooked GREAT NORTHERN BEANS
1 chopped ONION
1/2 lb. cooked HAM, cubed
1 (15 oz.) can PINEAPPLE CHUNKS, drained
1/2 cup packed BROWN SUGAR
1/2 cup KETCHUP
2 Tbsp. PREPARED MUSTARD

Combine ingredients together and mix well. Pour into a greased 13 x 9 x 2 inch baking dish. Cover and bake for 1 1/2 hours in a 350 degree oven. Uncover and bake for an additional 20 minutes.

Beans lend their texture and flavor to a wide variety of dishes.

Spanish Lentils

2 cups cooked LENTILS
1 chopped ONION
1 (15 oz.) can STEWED TOMATOES
1 chopped GREEN BELL PEPPER

2 Tbsp. OIL
1 tsp. OREGANO
1/2 tsp. SWEET BASIL
1/4 tsp. GARLIC SALT
1 1/2 tsp. CORNMEAL

Combine all of the ingredients in a skillet being careful that the cornmeal doesn't become lumpy. Simmer on low heat until onion and green pepper are tender.

Boston Baked Beans

1 lb. GREAT NORTHERN BEANS
6 strips chopped BACON
1 lg. chopped ONION
1 minced GARLIC CLOVE
3 Tbsp. BROWN SUGAR
2 Tbsp. DRY MUSTARD
2 Tbsp. WORCESTERSHIRE
   SAUCE
1/3 cup MOLASSES
3 Tbsp. CHILI SAUCE
5 Tbsp. KETCHUP
1/4 tsp. BLACK PEPPER
1/4 tsp. PAPRIKA
2 cups TOMATO JUICE

Soak beans in enough water to cover, overnight. Drain. Fry bacon in a large Dutch oven. When crisp, add onion and garlic. Sauté until onion is limp. Stir in remaining ingredients and mix thoroughly. Stir in the soaked, drained beans. Cover and bake in a 325 degree oven for 2 hours. Reduce temperature to 250 degrees and bake an additional 1 1/2 to 2 hours.

Boston has long been famous for baked beans. In fact, in the eighteenth century Boston was nicknamed "Beantown" due to its reknown as a center of outstanding baked bean recipes.

Zesty Limas

2 cups dried LIMA BEANS
1 chopped ONION
1 diced medium TOMATO
1 cup TOMATO PURÉE
2 minced GARLIC CLOVES
1/4 tsp. CAYENNE
1 tsp. SALT
PEPPER to taste

Wash and drain beans in a colander. Place limas in cooking pot and cover with water 4 inches above beans. Bring to a boil and reduce heat to medium-low, cooking for about 2 hours or until tender. Add more water if needed. During the last 1/2 hour of cooking, add the remaining ingredients.

Lima beans are in the kidney bean family. Two main types are available: the large, thick "potato" limas which are cream-colored and mellow-tasting and the small "baby" lima beans which are green.

Rice & Kidney Beans

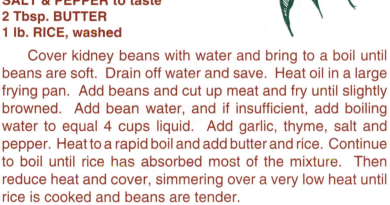

1 lb. dried KIDNEY BEANS
2 Tbsp. VEGETABLE OIL
SALT PORK, HAM or SAUSAGES
2 minced GARLIC CLOVES
1/2 tsp. THYME
SALT & PEPPER to taste
2 Tbsp. BUTTER
1 lb. RICE, washed

Cover kidney beans with water and bring to a boil until beans are soft. Drain off water and save. Heat oil in a large frying pan. Add beans and cut up meat and fry until slightly browned. Add bean water, and if insufficient, add boiling water to equal 4 cups liquid. Add garlic, thyme, salt and pepper. Heat to a rapid boil and add butter and rice. Continue to boil until rice has absorbed most of the mixture. Then reduce heat and cover, simmering over a very low heat until rice is cooked and beans are tender.

Beans can be soaked overnight or several hours prior to cooking. Do not salt soaking water as this will make the skin of the beans tough.

Lentils & Rice Casserole

1 cup dried LENTILS
1 cup uncooked RICE
1/4 cup BUTTER
4 chopped PLUMS
1 finely chopped ONION
1 chopped GREEN APPLE
1 tsp. SALT
1/2 tsp. CINNAMON

Preheat oven to 350 degrees. Cook lentils and rice separately as packages direct. Drain lentils and rice and toss together in a large bowl. In a skillet, melt butter and cook plums, onion and apple until soft. Add to lentil/rice mixture. Mix in remaining ingredients. Spoon into a greased 2-quart casserole and cover. Bake 40 minutes.

Colombian Black Beans

The milk floating on top makes this dish unique.

1 lb. dried BLACK BEANS
SALT to taste
2 Tbsp. COOKING OIL

1 chopped ONION
BLACK PEPPER to taste
MILK

Wash beans well and soak overnight in cold water. In the morning, drain and cover again with cold water. Slowly bring to boiling point. Add salt to taste and allow to simmer until beans are tender.

Heat cooking oil in a frying pan. Fry the chopped onion until it is browned. Add drained beans with a dash of black pepper. Turn beans in oil until coated. Add just enough milk to cover. Bring slowly to a boil and serve.

Bean Stuffing

For great Southwestern flavor, try this unique stuffing!

1 lb. CHORIZO (a spicy Mexican
   sausage)
1 lb. PORK SAUSAGE
1 chopped ONION
2 (15 oz.) cans PINTO BEANS, drained
1/4 tsp. GARLIC POWDER
3 Tbsp. minced, fresh PARSLEY
1 tsp. SAGE
1 (9 oz.) bag CORN CHIPS
   or TORTILLA CHIPS

Fry chorizo and sausage in a large skillet until thoroughly cooked. Drain very well. Sauté onions in the same frying pan. Return meats to pan and add beans, garlic powder, parsley and sage. Place chips in a large plastic bag, crush to break into small pieces. Add crushed chips to skillet and simmer all together for 15 minutes, stirring occasionally.

This recipe will stuff a 12-lb. turkey or can be baked in a greased casserole dish in a moderate oven until top is crispy and served as a side dish.

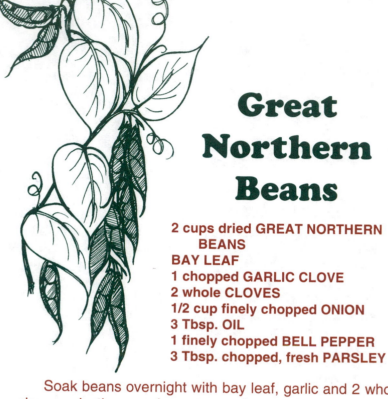

Great Northern Beans

2 cups dried GREAT NORTHERN BEANS
BAY LEAF
1 chopped GARLIC CLOVE
2 whole CLOVES
1/2 cup finely chopped ONION
3 Tbsp. OIL
1 finely chopped BELL PEPPER
3 Tbsp. chopped, fresh PARSLEY

Soak beans overnight with bay leaf, garlic and 2 whole cloves. In the morning, remove bay leaf and two whole cloves and cook beans in the same water until tender (about 2 hours). Brown onion in oil, add bell pepper and parsley and cook until tender. Add to the beans, mix thoroughly and serve.

Ham & Beans Aloha

1 (28 oz.) can BAKED BEANS
2 lb. fully cooked HAM STEAKS, cut into bite-size pieces
3 PINEAPPLE RINGS, cut in halves
2 Tbsp. BROWN SUGAR

In a 2-quart casserole, combine beans and ham. Top with the pineapple slices and sprinkle with the brown sugar. Bake, uncovered, at 350 degrees for 30 minutes.

Apple & Navy Bean Casserole

This is a great combination of flavors!

2 cups dried NAVY BEANS
6 cups cold WATER
1 tsp. SALT
3 large APPLES, peeled and sliced
3/4 cup BROWN SUGAR
1/2 tsp. CINNAMON
1 1/2 Tbsp. BUTTER

Wash beans and soak overnight to cut down on cooking time. Drain the soaking water and cover with the 6 cups cold water. Add salt and bring to a boil. Turn down the heat to a simmer, cover and cook for an hour and 30 minutes. Drain the beans. Layer the beans and apples in a greased 2-quart casserole dish. Sprinkle the brown sugar and cinnamon over each layer. Dot with butter, cover and bake for 1 1/2 hours at 300 degrees.

Remember, most beans will rehydrate to triple their size, so be sure to start with a large enough pot.

Hummus

Pronounced "hŭmmŭs"
this Middle-Eastern
favorite makes a great
spread for crackers.

2 cups cooked
   GARBANZO BEANS
1 GARLIC CLOVE
1/4 cup LEMON JUICE
1/4 cup OLIVE OIL
COLD WATER
FRESH PARSLEY

Purée first four ingredients in a food processor or blender. Add a little water, if needed to make mixture softer. Garnish with chopped fresh parsley on top and refrigerate for at least one hour before serving.

Bean Patties

2 cups cooked GREAT NORTHERN BEANS
1 tsp. APPLE CIDER VINEGAR
1 Tbsp. OIL
1/2 cup chopped ONION
1/2 tsp. OREGANO
2 Tbsp. chopped, fresh PARSLEY
1 EGG
CRACKER CRUMBS

Cook the beans and press through a food mill or sieve while still hot (they purée much better). Add remaining ingredients except for egg and cracker crumbs. Form bean mixture into patties, dip into beaten egg and then roll in cracker crumbs. Fry in hot oil or if you prefer, grease a baking pan with oil and bake at 425 degrees for 10 minutes or until brown, turning once. Serve hot!

Breads

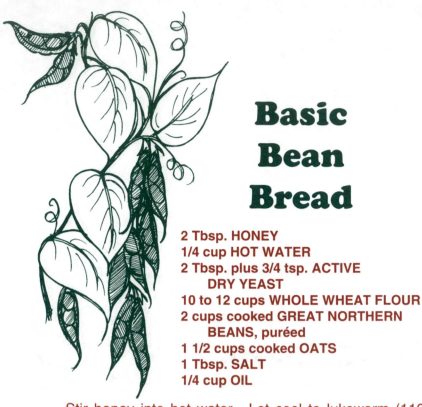

Basic Bean Bread

2 Tbsp. HONEY
1/4 cup HOT WATER
2 Tbsp. plus 3/4 tsp. ACTIVE
 DRY YEAST
10 to 12 cups WHOLE WHEAT FLOUR
2 cups cooked GREAT NORTHERN
 BEANS, puréed
1 1/2 cups cooked OATS
1 Tbsp. SALT
1/4 cup OIL

Stir honey into hot water. Let cool to lukewarm (110 degrees). Sprinkle in the yeast and mix to dissolve. Stir in 1 tablespoon of flour, cover and set aside for 10 minutes.

In a large bowl, combine beans, oats, salt and oil. Stir yeast mixture into bean mixture. Stir in enough whole wheat flour to form a stiff dough. If dough is too dry and crumbly, add water a tablespoon at a time until the desired consistency is achieved.

Turn dough out onto a floured surface and knead, working in additional flour as needed, until dough is smooth and elastic, approximately 15 minutes.

Oil your hands, rubbing over the surface of the dough. Cut dough into 4 equal pieces. Cover dough with clean towels, making sure that each piece has room to rise without touching others. Allow bread dough to rise for 45 minutes to 1 hour.

(Continued on next page)

Basic Bean Bread
(Continued from page 94)

Preheat oven to 375 degrees. Lightly oil bread pans. Shape dough into loaves and place in prepared pans. Bake until crust is golden, about 45 minutes. Remove bread from pans and place on wire racks. Let cool for at least 20 minutes before slicing.

This recipe will make four 1 1/2 lb. loaves.

Here are some more great breads to make with the Basic Bean Bread recipe!

Bean & Chile Loaf

Use the same **Basic Bean Bread** recipe on the previous page. Replace the **GREAT NORTHERN BEANS** with **PINTO BEANS**. Add **1 small can diced GREEN CHILES**.

Banana Nut Loaf

Use the same **Basic Bean Bread** recipe on the previous page. Add to the bean mixture:

2 mashed BANANAS
3/4 cup chopped WALNUTS

2 tsp. VANILLA
1/2 tsp. CINNAMON

Allow for extra baking time due to moisture content in bananas.

Bean-Oat Muffins

1 cup cooked PINTO BEANS
3/4 cup MILK
1 EGG
1/4 cup VEGETABLE OIL
1/2 cup HONEY
1/2 tsp. VANILLA
1 cup FLOUR
3/4 cup QUICK COOKING OATS
1/2 tsp. BAKING SODA
1/2 tsp. CINNAMON
1/2 cup RAISINS

Preheat oven to 400 degrees. Purée beans with milk in a blender until smooth. Pour into a bowl and beat in egg, oil, honey and vanilla. Add in the dry ingredients, mixing until just moistened. Stir in raisins. Spoon into paper-lined muffin cups, about 3/4 full. Bake for 15 to 20 minutes or until golden brown.

Cooking beans in a crockpot takes from 6 to 8 hours or overnight.

Garbanzo Crackers

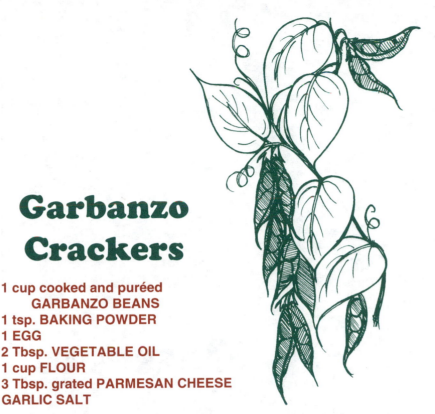

1 cup cooked and puréed
    GARBANZO BEANS
1 tsp. BAKING POWDER
1 EGG
2 Tbsp. VEGETABLE OIL
1 cup FLOUR
3 Tbsp. grated PARMESAN CHEESE
GARLIC SALT

    Preheat oven to 425 degrees. Combine all ingredients, but the garlic salt, with a fork or in a food processor until well blended. Roll out to 1/8 inch thick on a floured board. Score into 1 1/2 inch squares. Sprinkle with garlic salt and bake on a cookie sheet for 10 minutes or until golden brown. Cool and break apart at the scored lines.

Legumes provide protein, calcium, phosphorus, vitamins and other nutrients that are vital for good health.

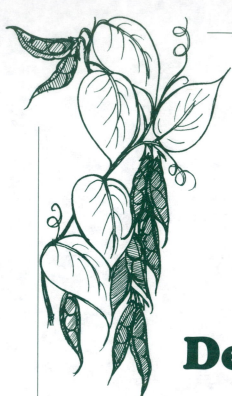

Desserts

Baking
with Beans

Baking with puréed beans can be achieved by using your own home cooked beans or by using canned beans. If you are using your cooked beans, make sure they are well cooked and very tender with no flavorings added to the cooking water. Drain the beans thoroughly. Purée in a food processor until they reach a smooth and creamy consistency. If you are using canned beans, (they work perfectly fine) be sure to rinse and drain the beans thoroughly.

Baking with beans makes for a more moist and nutritious delight. Allow for longer baking times due to the added water content in the bean purée.

Bean & Banana Cookies

1 cup BROWN SUGAR
2 EGGS
1/2 cup BUTTER
1/2 tsp. VANILLA
3/4 cup cooked and puréed
   NAVY BEANS
1 mashed BANANA
1 tsp. BAKING SODA
1 3/4 cup FLOUR
1/2 cup QUICK COOKING OATS
1 cup CHOCOLATE CHIPS

Preheat oven to 375 degrees. Cream sugar, eggs, butter and vanilla together. Add beans and banana and beat until fluffy. Add baking soda, flour and oats. Blend till smooth. Stir in chocolate chips. Drop by teaspoonful onto greased cookie sheet. Bake for 15-20 minutes or until golden brown.

Try substituting raisins for the chocolate chips or add walnuts or pecans for a different taste.

Soybean Pie

*This pie tastes very much
like pumpkin pie.*

1 1/2 cups well-cooked
    SOYBEANS
3/4 cup HONEY
1 tsp. CINNAMON
1/2 tsp. GINGER
3/4 tsp. NUTMEG
2 slightly beaten EGGS
3/4 cup MILK
PREPARED PIE CRUST

    Preheat oven to 450 degrees. Purée
soybeans in a blender or food processor. Combine with remaining ingredients except for the pie crust and pour
into crust. Bake for 15 minutes, then
reduce heat to 350 degrees and bake
for an additional 30 minutes or until
knife comes out clean. Delicious served
with whipped topping.

Lentil Brownies

1/2 cup LENTILS
4 EGGS
2 cups SUGAR
1 cup SALAD OIL
2 tsp. VANILLA

1 1/2 cups FLOUR
1 1/2 cup plus 2 Tbsp. COCOA
1 tsp. SALT
1 cup CHOCOLATE CHIPS
1 cup MARSHMALLOWS

    Cook lentils for 40 minutes and drain well. Beat the eggs
and sugar. Add in the oil and vanilla. Sift dry ingredients and
add to the sugar mixture. Stir in the lentils, chocolate chips
and marshmallows. Bake in a 9 x 13 pan at 350 degrees for
35 minutes.

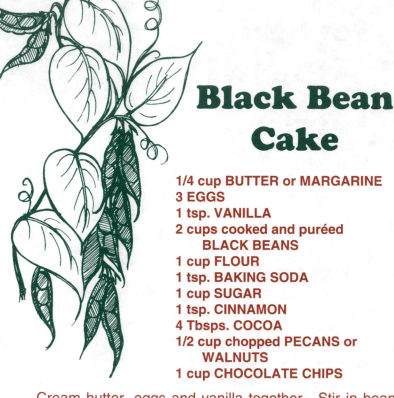

Black Bean Cake

1/4 cup BUTTER or MARGARINE
3 EGGS
1 tsp. VANILLA
2 cups cooked and puréed
    BLACK BEANS
1 cup FLOUR
1 tsp. BAKING SODA
1 cup SUGAR
1 tsp. CINNAMON
4 Tbsps. COCOA
1/2 cup chopped PECANS or
    WALNUTS
1 cup CHOCOLATE CHIPS

Cream butter, eggs and vanilla together. Stir in bean purée and beat well. Add all of the dry ingredients and combine thoroughly. Fold in the chopped nuts and chocolate chips. Pour into a greased 9 x 13 inch cake pan and bake at 375 degrees for 45-50 minutes. Frost with your favorite icing.

Navy Bean Pie

2 cups cooked, mashed
    NAVY BEANS
1 cup sugar
1/2 stick BUTTER, softened

3/4 tsp. VANILLA
1/4 tsp. CINNAMON
2 EGGS, well beaten
unbaked PIE CRUST

Thoroughly blend all ingredients and place in pie crust. Bake for 10 minutes at 425 degrees, and then 30 more minutes at 325 degrees. Let cool before slicing.

Pinto Bean Fudge

1 cup cooked and mashed PINTO BEANS
3/4 cup softened BUTTER
3/4 cup COCOA
1 Tbsp. VANILLA
1/2 cup chopped WALNUTS
2 lbs. POWDERED SUGAR

Combine beans, butter, cocoa and vanilla together. Stir in nuts and powdered sugar. Batter will be stiff. Spread into a buttered 9 x 13 inch pan. When thoroughly chilled, cut in squares. Store in the refrigerator.

Pinto Bean Cookies

1 cup cooked and puréed PINTO BEANS
2 EGGS
1 cup SUGAR
1/2 cup BUTTER, softened
2 cups FLOUR
1 tsp. BAKING SODA
1/2 tsp. SALT
1/2 tsp. CINNAMON
1 cup chopped NUTS
1 cup RAISINS

Preheat oven to 350 degrees. In a large mixing bowl, combine puréed beans, eggs, sugar and butter. Sift together the flour, baking soda, salt and cinnamon and blend into the bean mixture. Stir in the nuts and raisins. Drop by teaspoonful on a greased cookie sheet and bake for 15 minutes.

Spiced Bean Cake

2 cups BISCUIT MIX
1 1/2 cups SUGAR
1 tsp. CINNAMON
1/2 tsp. ALLSPICE
1/2 tsp. NUTMEG
1/3 cup softened BUTTER
2 EGGS
3/4 cup MILK
1 1/2 cups REFRIED BEANS
1/2 cup RAISINS
1/2 cup chopped NUTS

Preheat oven to 350 degrees. Combine biscuit mix, sugar, cinnamon, alspice and nutmeg. Add butter, eggs, and 1/4 cup milk. Mix at medium speed until well blended. Add refried beans, remaining milk, raisins and nuts. Beat well by hand and pour into a greased 8 x 8 x 2 pan. Bake in 350 degree oven for one hour or until firm. Serve warm or let cool and frost with *Creamy Frosting.*

Creamy Frosting

Add enough **WHIPPING CREAM** to 1 1/2 cups of **POWDERED SUGAR** to achieve a spreading consistency. Add 1/2 tsp. **VANILLA** 1/4 tsp. **CINNAMON** and a dash of **SALT**.

Harvest Cookies

1/4 cup LENTILS, rinsed
1 1/2 cups WATER
2 EGGS
1/2 cup HONEY
1/4 cup MARGARINE
1 tsp. VANILLA
1/3 cup canned PUMPKIN
1 cup unbleached FLOUR

1 cup WHOLE WHEAT FLOUR
3/4 tsp. SALT
2 tsp. BAKING POWDER
1/4 tsp. NUTMEG
1/4 tsp. GINGER
1 cup coarsely chopped
    WALNUTS
1/2 cup RAISINS

Combine the lentils with the water in a saucepan, and bring to a boil; reduce heat, cover, and simmer for 30 minutes, or until tender. Drain off excess liquid. In a large bowl, beat the eggs and add in the honey and margarine. Cream until smooth. Add the vanilla, pumpkin, and cooked lentils. In a separate bowl, combine the remaining ingredients except walnuts and raisins. Add the flour mixture and mix well. Add the walnuts and raisins. Drop dough onto a greased cookie sheet and bake for 10 minutes at 350 degrees.

Bean & Lentil Festivals

Texas — Black-Eyed Pea Fall Harvest — Athens (annual), 3rd weekend in October.   800-755-7878

California — California Dry Bean Festival — Tracy (annual), 1st full weekend in August.   209-835-2131
http://www.traceychamber.org.

Washington — National Lentil Festival — Pullman (annual), last weekend in August.   800-365-6948

Colorado — Pueblo Chile & Frijole Festival — Pueblo (annual), late September.   719-542-1704

Arkansas — Mountain View Bean Fest — Mountain View (annual), last weekend in October.   870-269-8068

Michigan — Bean Festival — Fairgrove, Labor Day Weekend
517-673-5211

Idaho — Filer Bean Festival — Filer, late March 208-334-3520

Index

About the Author

An exercise enthusiast, **Shayne Fischer** combines her interest in foods that taste good with a desire to create recipes that are nutritious and healthy. "Most of us would live longer and happier lives if we paid more attention to what we eat and to getting regular, beneficial exercise."

Shayne was born and still lives in Arizona. Active in the family publishing business (Golden West Publishers) and community affairs, she and her husband, Lee, find time for power walking, running, bicycling and hiking. She has also authored *Low Fat Mexican Recipes, Wholly Frijoles!* and *Vegi-Mex: Vegetarian Mexican Recipes.*

More Cook Books from Golden West Publishers

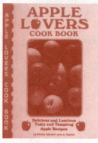

APPLE LOVERS COOK BOOK

Celebrating America's favorite—the apple! 150 recipes for main and side dishes, appetizers, salads, breads, muffins, cakes, pies desserts, beverages, and preserves, all kitchen-tested by Shirley Munson and Jo Nelson.

5 1/2 x 8 1/2 — 120 Pages . . . $6.95

PECAN LOVERS COOK BOOK

Indulge your pecan passion for pralines, macaroons, ice cream, bread pudding, rolls, muffins, cakes and cookies, main dishes and a wide variety of tantalizing pecan pies. By Mark Blazek.

5 1/2 x 8 1/2 — 120 Pages . . . $6.95

PUMPKIN LOVERS COOK BOOK

It's pumpkin time again! More than 175 recipes for soups, breads, muffins, pies, cakes, cheesecakes, cookies, ice cream, and more! Includes pumpkin trivia!

5 1/2 x 8 1/2—128 Pages . . . $6.95

TORTILLA LOVERS COOK BOOK

From tacos to tostadas, enchiladas to nachos, every dish celebrates the tortilla! More than 70 easy to prepare, festive recipes for breakfast, lunch and dinner. Filled with Southwestern flavors! By Bruce and Bobbi Fischer.

5 1/2 x 8 1/2 — 112 pages . . . $6.95

SALSA LOVERS COOK BOOK

More than 180 taste-tempting recipes for salsas that will make every meal a special event! Salsas for salads, appetizers, main dishes and desserts! Put some salsa in your life! By Susan K. Bollin. More than 200,000 copies in print!

5 1/2 x 8 1/2—128 pages . . . $5.95

More Cook Books from Golden West Publishers

CORN LOVERS COOK BOOK

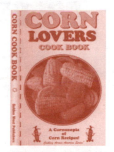

Over 100 delicious recipes featuring America's favorite! Try *Corn Chowder, Corn Soufflé, Apple Cornbread* or *Caramel Corn,* to name a few. You will find a tempting recipe for every occasion in this collection. Includes corn facts and trivia too!

5 1/2 x 8 1/2 — 88 pages . . . $6.95

THE JOY OF MUFFINS
The International Muffin Cook Book

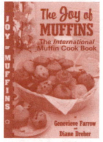

Recipes for *German Streusel, Finnish Cranberry, Italian Amaretto, Greek Baklava, Chinese Almond, Jamaican Banana, Swiss Fondue,* microwave section and ten recipes for oat bran muffins . . . 50 recipes in all!

5 1/2 x 8 1/2 — 120 Pages . . . $5.95

VEGGIE LOVERS COOK BOOK

Everyone will love these no-cholesterol, no-animal recipes! Over 200 nutritious, flavorful recipes by Chef Morty Star. Includes a foreword by Dr. Michael Klaper. Nutritional analysis for each recipe to help you plan a healthy diet.

5 1/2 x 8 1/2 — 128 pages . . . $6.95

CHIP & DIP LOVERS
COOK BOOK

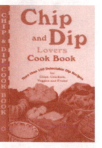

More than 150 recipes for fun and festive dips. Make southwestern dips, dips with fruits and vegetables, meats, poultry and seafood. Salsa dips and dips for desserts. Includes recipes for making homemade chips. By Susan K. Bollin.

5 1/2 x 8 1/2—112 pages . . . $5.95

BEST BARBECUE RECIPES

A collection of more than 200 taste-tempting recipes. • Sauces • Rubs • Marinades • Mops • Ribs • Wild Game • Fish and Seafood • Pit barbecue and more! By Mildred Fischer.

5 1/2 x 8 1/2 — 144 pages . . . $5.95

ORDER BLANK

GOLDEN WEST PUBLISHERS

☼ 4113 N. Longview Ave. • Phoenix, AZ 85014

602-265-4392 • **1-800-658-5830** • FAX 602-279-6901

Qty	Title	Price	Amount
	Apple Lovers Cook Book	**6.95**	
	Bean Lovers Cook Book	**6.95**	
	Best Barbecue Recipes	**5.95**	
	Chili-Lovers' Cook Book	**5.95**	
	Chip and Dip Lovers Cook Book	**5.95**	
	Corn Lovers Cook Book	**6.95**	
	Iowa Cook Book	**6.95**	
	Joy of Muffins	**5.95**	
	Low Fat Mexican Recipes	**6.95**	
	Mexican Desserts & Drinks	**6.95**	
	Pecan Lovers Cook Book	**6.95**	
	Pumpkin Lovers Cook Book	**6.95**	
	Quick-n-Easy Mexican Recipes	**5.95**	
	Real New Mexico Chile	**6.95**	
	Salsa Lovers Cook Book	**5.95**	
	Take This Chile & Stuff It!	**6.95**	
	Tortilla Lovers Cook Book	**6.95**	
	Veggie Lovers Cook Book	**6.95**	
	Vegi-Mex: Vegetarian Mexican Recipes	**6.95**	
	Western Breakfasts	**7.95**	

| Shipping & Handling Add ➠ | U.S. & Canada | $3.00 | |
| | Other countries | $5.00 | |

☐ My Check or Money Order Enclosed $

☐ MasterCard   ☐ VISA ($20 credit card minimum)

(Payable in U.S. funds)

Acct. No.   Exp. Date

Signature

Name   Telephone

Address

City/State/Zip   **Call for FREE catalog**   Bean Lovers

6/99

This order form may be copied and faxed or mailed.